Eat Your Yard!

Eat Your Yard!

Edible trees, shrubs, vines, herbs and flowers for your landscape

NAN K. CHASE

GIBBS SMITH

TO ENRICH AND INSPIRE HUMANKIND

Salt Lake City | Charleston | Santa Fe | Santa Barbara

First Edition
14 13 12 11 10   5 4 3 2 1

Text © 2010 Nan K. Chase
Photographs © 2010 as noted throughout
Cover photographs: *front top* by Lori Cannon; *front left* courtesy of Northwest Cherry Growers; *front center* by heidi@heidiswanson.com; *front right* by Robin Siktberg for the Herb Society of America; *front flap* courtesy of The California Fruit Tree Agreement; *back flap* by Lonnie Webster; *back cover, right,* by iStock-Photo/lucylui; *back cover, top left,* by Michelle Levy Brocco, www.mishmishcards.com; *back cover, bottom left,* by Henry Firus of Flagstaffotos, Australia

Published by
Gibbs Smith
P.O. Box 667
Layton, Utah 84041

Orders: 1.800.835.4993
www.gibbs-smith.com

Designed by Jocelyn Foye
Printed and bound in China
Gibbs Smith books are printed on either recycled, 100% post-consumer waste, or FSC-certified papers.

Library of Congress Cataloging-in-Publication Data

Chase, Nan K., 1954-
  Eat your yard! : edible trees, shrubs, vines, herbs and flowers for your landscape / Nan K. Chase. — 1st ed.
    p. cm.
  Includes index.
  ISBN-13: 978-1-4236-0384-9
  ISBN-10: 1-4236-0384-2
  1. Plants, Edible. 2. Edible landscaping. I. Title.
  QK98.5.A1 C45 2010
  635—dc22
                                2009032716

For my parents, Peter and Dorothy Koltnow, who took me to Fresno, where the fruit trees grow

And for Saul Chase, my rock for forty years

ACKNOWLEDGEMENTS

Dozens of individuals and organizations around the world made generous contributions toward this book, including trade and agricultural organizations, government agencies and universities, commercial nurseries and manufacturers, amateur growers and professional botanists, photographers, celebrity chefs, and bloggers. Their names are woven into the narrative and the recipes, and appear in the Resources section. These people and groups are noteworthy for having supplied many of the outstanding photographs and mouthwatering recipes in this book. I thank them all for sharing.

In addition, I thank Jamie Goodman of Boone, North Carolina. Without her technical assistance and critical eye, this book would not have been possible.

Contents

Photo courtesy of David Austin Roses.

Introduction

I love the fact that my yard feeds me. It's a lush and colorful landscape, but it's also designed with eating in mind. In this edible landscape, there's usually something ripe; and when the weather grows cold, my cupboards and freezer are filled with the rest of the harvest.

The edible yard combines beauty and practicality: beautiful form in the garden with bounteous crops to eat fresh or preserve for year-round enjoyment.

I'm not interested in ripping out the front lawn to plant zucchini and tomatoes. Sure, both those plants are useful to grow, but where's the beauty? How does that summer-green tangle look in the dead of winter?

No, I propose a new way to visualize and plan a home garden, no matter the size. A way to use the garden more efficiently than ever, both to add definition, color, and texture to garden space and to maximize garden space for food production.

I want to give gardeners all over North America new ideas about the many beautiful trees, shrubs, vines, herbs, and wildflowers that also produce delicious fruits and other edible components (nuts, seeds, leaves, flowers, and tuberous roots).

This book contains more than thirty such plants or plant groupings, from apples to yucca, and I describe the most attractive design features of each: autumn leaf color, for instance, or winter interest, or spectacular flowers.

For each of these plants I also supply a recipe or two—something mouthwatering, or something to "put up" for winter, or new ways to use familiar foods, or new foods to try for the first time.

In choosing the mix of recipes, I looked for opportunities to enjoy the foods at meals throughout the day, to use multiple plants

Fruit blossoms like these delicate flowers are a feast for the eyes in early spring, but they must be tough enough to withstand rain and snow. Photo by Nan K. Chase.

in as many recipes as possible, and to preserve surplus in volume. All inspiration, I hope, for taking on the challenges of creating and utilizing an edible landscape.

My passion for growing edible plants in the landscape began long, long before the recent move toward locally grown food. My first encounters came more than fifty years ago, when I was still a toddler living in California. Our backyard was filled with fruit trees, and we kids took plums and almonds right off the branches as soon as we could climb up and get them.

Since then I have lived in Maryland and Wisconsin and have studied gardens in England, France, Hungary, and, most spectacularly, the former Yugoslavia; there, on the Adriatic Coast in 1990, my husband, Saul, and I stayed with a family whose small front yard was so densely packed with berry bushes, plum trees, and other edible plants that it fed an extended family of ten people. They lived in a small town, not on a farm, and yet they ate like royalty from a few square feet.

Is there any reason that the people living in our vast American suburbs, with their quarter-acre and half-acre lots, could not feed themselves, that we could not slash our country's energy needs and food expenditures at the same time that we enhance our home landscapes?

For nearly the last thirty years I have lived and gardened in western North Carolina, and by now have tried, with varying degrees of success, to grow almost every plant listed in this book. Name it, I have it (except, currently, an olive, kumquat, almond, or pecan tree).

They haven't all thrived, of course. Some trees never made it to year two, but others have produced steadily from the first season. By having a few specimens of lots of different edible landscape plants, my family has been able to enjoy a range of delicious, super-nutritious and organic foods from the yard: crabapple jelly and blueberry jam all winter, fresh greens in spring, grapes and apples and pears in summer, and soon, I hope, pawpaws in the fall. (Yes, I grow tomatoes and kale and squash, too, but they and the other kitchen crops of summer have their own low-profile territory in my yard.)

As for landscape beauty—there's no question these edible plants are both functional and beautiful; the nut trees, the berry bushes, the herbs, the vines, and the wildflowers all add richness to the outdoor experience and to the views from indoors.

Mostly the edible landscape takes time, an investment of day-to-day attention, plus a willingness to drop everything else for a day or two when the harvest comes in. Should you be lucky enough to have a big crop, preserve as much as possible. Learn to can, dry, or freeze foods. It's not difficult. It just takes a commitment—the choice—of time.

This book describes a relatively few edible landscape plants; the range of possibilities from around the world is too large to embrace in one volume of this size. I have selected the plants that I feel have the greatest landscape value for the greatest number of gardeners, and which have the greatest potential food enjoyment with a moderate amount of work.

I garden informally, having discovered that zones are meant to be stretched. Try taking advantage of microclimates in your own yard—even if it's just a patio or balcony—to expand your plant holdings. Most of the plants in this book grow in most of the country.

Good luck, and get started today!

A FEW WORDS ABOUT ORGANIC GARDENING

For many gardeners there simply is no alternative to organic gardening, and I have grown almost all of my crops organically with great success and little bother. Even fruit trees, which sometimes require pest control, can be sprayed with organic compounds.

If you haven't gardened before, or if you hope to improve the health of your garden (and your family), now is a good time to incorporate a few fundamental practices that can lessen dependence on harsh or dangerous chemical treatments.

The best way to nurture an organic garden is to invite birds into it. Install a birdbath—not a bird feeder—and keep it full. Plant lots of different flowering species. Birds need water, and once they arrive in your yard they will find plenty of food naturally. Birds will groom your plants, removing many insect pests as they feed and aerating the ground as they hunt for more.

It's also important to build and maintain healthy soil. With enough organic additives, even the hardest clay can be turned into rich, friable loam in a few years. When confronted with poor soil I have added lots of greensand (a natural soil conditioner), bone meal, blood meal, manure (or kelp meal or fish fertilizer), composted yard and kitchen waste, yet more greensand, and then topped it all with mulch.

To help your fruit-bearing plants, be sure to keep the soil around them weeded and free from suffocating vines, and dig all around to aerate the soil and discourage harmful funguses.

Favorite Fruits

He's the apple of my eye . . .
    Skin like peaches and cream . . .
Lips like cherry wine . . .

The language of fruit, like fruit itself, is sensual, luscious, almost drunken in its excess. It drips with desire, with sweetness, but sometimes includes a tart crunch, an unexpected bite of flavor.

This complex ripeness of fruit in its natural-grown state comes to us only part of the year, and we crave it. We picture then not the cold uniformity of a grocery store produce aisle at some indeterminate season, but the surprising warmth of fruit plucked right off the tree at the peak of its succulence.

Growing orchard fruits surely ranks as one of the most rewarding of garden experiences, one that spans generations and links us to the ancient past, as well as tying us to the unknowable but hopeful future.

There's a tremendous sense of accomplishment in planting a young fruit tree, watching it grow to bearing size, and then enjoying and preserving the bounteous fruit in its many forms.

Luck, hard work, and patience are requisites of the endeavor, of course, so using orchard fruits in the home garden is a process of learning over many years, a humbling experience that deepens and unfolds oh so gradually.

After all, fruit trees are like children: they need sunshine and fresh air, dry feet, balanced nutrition, and an occasional haircut. Then they'll grow up big and strong.

When we plant fruit trees in the home landscape we get to watch up close the pageant of procreation: the love-making dance between insect and plant, the drama of the elements, growth and decay, life and death in an unwavering and unmerciful annual cycle.

Consider the rewards as you begin growing orchard crops: superior flavor and nutrition from organically grown trees, such as this Callaway Crab, in your own back or front yard. Photo by Nan K. Chase.

Photo courtesy of the California Tree Fruit Agreement.

And we get to watch as the infant fruit takes hold, growing ever larger with summer's heat and rain and with tending, as it approaches the moment of harvest, the long, slow climax of summer.

All that sensuality of the fruit ignores the great value of orchard trees in the home landscape. One needn't have acres of open land in order to enjoy the scenic enhancements. No, the most wonderful orchard crops can also add greatly to a modest-sized yard in the form of individual or, at most, paired specimen trees (requirements for pollination vary). Just a few small, carefully situated, faithfully pruned and weeded fruit trees can do two important jobs: provide a bounty of fruit to be "put up" for the winter and add the drama of massed pink or white blossoms to the home landscape in early spring.

Spring certainly brings out the best in our favorite fruit trees, which produce wands of light, fresh, finely veined blossoms reaching for the sky (or, as cuttings kept in a vase, brightening the living room). But with the most beloved orchard crops, there are also scenes of timeless enjoyment in midsummer as one sits conversing with family and friends beneath the dense, ripening boughs, cool and tranquil together within imaginary summer-houses of shade. And all that after only three or four years!

In fall, modest bursts of color play back and forth across the home landscape, and then in winter, the fine, open profiles of favorite fruit trees continue to delight us when all the supposedly strong and stalwart perennial plants have frozen and wilted into the ground. Snow collects from time to time in the limbs. Birds pass through and perch, but, mostly, the trees wait for spring.

Apple

If any plant can talk, it's the apple.

"Take me! Take me!" it shouts. "I'm wonderful!"

Why shouldn't the apple brag? It's one of the healthiest foods anywhere, with the power to fight cancer and heart disease, improve memory, and make the lungs work better. Apples are delicious and fun to eat, and they come in hundreds of varieties for many tastes and climates.

Robust fruit production requires good air circulation through the trees, healthy soil with adequate moisture, and seasonal pruning to prevent excess limb growth. Photo courtesy of U.S. Apple Association/S. Haaga.

Apple trees are among the happiest of trees; not carefree, but stupendously productive and lovely in the garden once established. The addition of two or three apple trees of different types in the home landscape—more if space allows—will provide ample rewards for your time.

There's no comparison between a bland, waxy supermarket apple and one that's ripe off the tree at home. Just one successful crop and you'll never want another store-bought apple.

Caution: Don't plant apple trees unless you're ready to can, dehydrate, ferment, or otherwise process the surplus fruit. It would be a shame to let such bounty go to waste. A young apple tree takes some years to get established before the internal structure

German Pancake

Boiling water

1/2 to 3/4 cup chopped dried apples, apricots, cherries, dates, figs,
 pears, raisins, or dried currants

6 tablespoons butter

6 eggs

1 cup milk

1 teaspoon sugar

1/4 teaspoon salt

1/2 teaspoon vanilla extract

1 cup flour

Lemon juice and powdered sugar or berry jam or jelly, if desired

Pour boiling water over dried fruit to cover. Let stand to soften 5
to 15 minutes; drain. Preheat oven to 400 degrees F (205 degrees C).
In preheating oven, melt butter in a 9 x 13-inch baking pan, checking
frequently to avoid scorching. In a blender, combine eggs, milk, sugar, salt,
and vanilla. Blend lightly to mix.

Add flour. Mix well in blender. With a wooden spoon or rubber
spatula, stir in fruit. Pour into baking pan containing melted butter. Bake
20 to 25 minutes, until puffy and golden brown. If desired, sprinkle with
lemon juice and powdered sugar or serve with berry jam or jelly. Serve
immediately. Makes 4 to 6 servings.

Recipe "German Pancake," from How to Dry Foods, Revised Edition, *by Deanna
DeLong, ©2006 by Deanna DeLong. Used by permission of Berkley Publishing Group,
a division of Penguin Group (USA) Inc.*

can support fruit production. But a healthy apple tree may live for a
century and bear fruit heavily for forty or fifty years of that—sometimes a hundred pounds or more a season.

A member of the rose family, the apple is close kin to pears and
quinces. It has been cultivated for thousands of years, in western
Asia at first, thence to Europe and North America.

LANDSCAPE HIGHLIGHTS
- Spring blossoms
- Summer and fall harvest

EDIBLE HIGHLIGHTS
- Fresh fruit from the tree
- Canned as applesauce, apple butter, spiced apples juice, or cider
- Dehydrated in slices

WHERE IT GROWS BEST
- In temperate zones with cold winters
- In full sun
- In a fertile, well-drained soil

HOW TO GROW IT
- With specific local characteristics (see Resources section for Agricultural Extension information)
- With other apple varieties for cross-pollination and longer harvest period
- With plenty of moisture
- With moderate pruning for air circulation and height
- Use apples in the landscape for impressive displays of white and pink springtime flowers.
- In a small yard, place a semi-dwarf variety at the far edge as a focal point to "expand" the vista, or in the middle of the yard as an anchor for a flower bed.
- In a large suburban or country yard, semi-dwarf or standard-size varieties can be massed along a fence, with adequate spacing.
- In a very small yard or patio setting, use one of the new columnar varieties for mostly vertical growth.

HARDINESS ZONES
North America is divided into eleven climate zones, numbered 1–11, with Zone 1 the coldest and Zone 11 the warmest. Minimum temperatures are noted in 10-degree F increments.

While zones don't tell the whole story of what will grow and thrive, they help in choosing varieties for your locality. See the zone finder on the National Gardening Association's website, www.garden.org.

Usually orchard trees need some frost to produce fruit, although frost-free apples are under development. Some apples grow in -30 degrees F, Zone 4.

Photo by Nan K. Chase.

Today, breeders are expanding the traditional range of apples to include warmer climates. There are apple trees specially suited to all temperate regions of the United States, with some surviving even at -30° F. And there's a resurgence of interest in planting heirloom varieties with superior taste.

The best approach to growing apple trees, then, is to begin close to home. That's where the United States Department of Agriculture's Cooperative Extension System comes in. With offices in each state, the Extension provides free educational advice and materials for home gardeners and others. The Web resources are excellent, but a phone call or visit to a local Ag Extension agent provides the most locally relevant information, including plant suppliers.

Horticultural "tech support" is especially important with apples, almost all of which combine root stock from one kind of plant with the fruiting upper part of another in a graft. Knowing which varieties—which grafts—favor the many mini-climates of the Northwest, the Midwest, the Northeast, and the South requires research and experience.

Then there's the matter of size: dwarf, semi-dwarf, or standard. Each has its growth and fruiting characteristics, its typical lifespan, and its particular place in the culinary world. And there are complex pollination requirements, so consult the experts first and save a lot of time and guesswork.

Or do what I did: ignore all sensible advice, plant what you find close to home and on sale, and hope for the best. My random young trees—a mix of Jonagold and Jonared apples—have responded to the rough mountain weather with bumper crops.

Cherry

The cherry tree is garden royalty, a horticultural grand duchess of regal stature and luxuriant garb, dispensing gifts liberally . . . but, like royalty, occasionally withholding her favors.

Among the first orchard trees to blossom in the spring and the first to bear fruit (and bearing younger than most other fruit trees), the cherry deserves a prominent place in the edible

Preserving cherries is a pleasure once you've had your fill of fresh fruit. Canning, drying, or freezing ripe cherries can liven up the winter table at low cost. Photo courtesy of Northwest Cherry Growers.

landscape. The cherry tree in magnificent bloom has come, over centuries of art history, to represent the visual essence of purity, beauty, and hope. Imagine how much more intense is the springtime experience of a cherry tree in full bloom when it occurs in your own home landscape.

To add to the allure, blossoming time often overlaps with snow, producing moody compositions of turbulent grey skies and snow-covered pink petals.

Beauty persists through an exceptionally long harvest season, ranging from June to August, depending on variety, and then through the red-gold glory days of autumn and into the winter months, when cherry bark gleams with warmth and color against crystalline snow. Soon after that, the flowers come again.

Savory Cherry Sauce

1 tablespoon butter
2 tablespoons minced shallots
1¼ cups canned sweet cherries, drained*
½ cup Pinot Noir
½ cup chicken stock or low-sodium broth
½ teaspoon fresh thyme leaves
1 teaspoon cornstarch dissolved in 1 teaspoon water

Melt butter in a medium saucepan. Add shallots and cook until golden brown, about 5 minutes. Stir in cherries, wine, and broth. Simmer 15 minutes over medium heat. Let cool slightly; then puree in a blender or food processor. Return to pan and add thyme and cornstarch. Whisk constantly over medium-low heat for 10 to 15 minutes, or until thickened and reduced to about ¾ cup.

Recipe courtesy of National Cherry Growers & Industries Foundation.

*Canned sweet cherries are made using fresh cherries packed in a hot syrup of 1½ cups sugar to 2 cups water, and then sealed in sterile pint or quart jars with a 25-minute boiling water bath.

A well-placed cherry tree becomes the focal point of an edible landscape, providing four seasons of beauty in addition to superb fruit. Photo ©iStockPhoto/ Marie Fields.

The fruit of the cherry tree is treasured for its voluptuous sweetness and satisfying texture. Cherries have important properties: high levels of anti-inflammatory and pain-killing compounds, potassium, sleep-regulating melatonin, and antioxidants. The fresh fruit is a pleasure to eat, and it also lends itself to canning and dehydration for year-round enjoyment.

Cherry trees don't need much pruning or fertilizer. The lustrous wood glows red and is used for fine furniture, cabinets, and musical instruments. Not a bad use of a fine old tree once its bearing days are over.

Cherry trees have a few big drawbacks. Some kinds of cherries are more tender than others, so plant selection is important. Some are susceptible to insect pests and diseases. And, not insignificantly, a

LANDSCAPE HIGHLIGHTS
- Spring blossoms
- Winter bark interest

EDIBLE HIGHLIGHTS
- Fresh fruit from the tree
- Canned (pitted) as pie filling or sauce
- Dehydrated (pitted) for snacks
- Frozen for winter use

WHERE IT GROWS BEST
- In a cool or cold climate (to -40 degrees F, Zone 3)
- In deeply worked friable soil that drains well
- In full sun

HOW TO GROW IT
- With some cross-pollination; check variety for requirements
- With bird netting to protect fruit (see Bird Netting, this page)
- With planting in fall or early spring
- On dwarf root stock for ease of harvest
- Near decorative borders or comfortable seating
- Situated in a raked gravel bed for a tranquil Asian feel

BIRD NETTING
Especially delicious fruit crops attract flocks of birds, so many gardeners install medium-weight bird netting over the fruiting trees or bushes before fruit ripens. Methods may include netting alone or on a framework of plastic piping or wood. The reusable nets are widely available at farm or home improvement stores, or online. Lightweight or fine netting is hard to handle. Some gardeners build movable chicken wire boxes to guard low-growing fruit or nuts.

Photo courtesy of Northwest Cherry Growers.

season's fruit can quickly be wiped out by hungry birds, so you'll need netting every year if harvest is a prime goal. Heavy rains too close to harvest can ruin the fruit, and fruit may not set at all if blossoms are knocked off by a storm.

Nonetheless, the cherry tree grows well in conditions found widely throughout the United States and remains a garden favorite.

There are three categories of cherry: sweet cherries, sour (or pie) cherries, and hybrid types, sometimes referred to as Duke cherries.

Generally the sweet cherries are the big juicy kinds that grace local fruit stands and make their way into supermarkets. These trees are more tender than the sour cherries, more like peaches in their requirements for mild weather and careful pest control.

Sweet cherry trees are taller and broader and are more difficult to protect from birds in the home landscape unless grown on dwarf or semi-dwarf stock. They need cross-pollination, whereas the sour cherries are generally self-fertile.

The sour cherries can withstand more cold (try -40° F), more bugs, more neglect, and soil that's not as deeply worked or as rich. They aren't really sour but are widely used in cooking, as they are flavorful and juicy and not overly sweet. And some nutrient levels are higher for the sour varieties.

Hybrids have characteristics of both, in varying proportions, and can be advantageous in meeting the challenges of particular locations. Just as with apples, this is a time to do research for local plant sources through your nearest Agricultural Extension office.

Thoughtful placement of cherry trees, particularly the more sensitive sweet cherries, can help the chances of success: a location at the side of a pond or a lake, or on a hillside, can mitigate the effects of a late freeze.

Crabapple

Surprise! The crabapple is a must-have tree in the edible landscape.

Smaller than most other fruit trees and hardy to sub-Arctic temperatures, the crabapple needs little care yet reliably produces loads of delicious fruit that's packed with vitamin C and pectin, and therefore perfect for making jelly. The jelly is truly "summer in a jar" thanks to its sunny hue, and it makes a treat

Crabapples reflect the changing colors of early autumn as they ripen. Unpicked fruit remains on the tree as wildlife food through the winter. Photo © iStockPhoto/Stuart Brill.

in midwinter. (Some cooks add crabapple juice to their apple cider in the fall for extra flavor.)

Crabapple trees encourage good pollination for other kinds of apples and should be used for that reason alone. Any late-summer fruit that isn't harvested will stay on the trees for months, providing food for wildlife.

And then there are the flowers in spring, in shades from snow white to magenta, a great addition to the landscape.

I don't know where the crabapple's unfavorable reputation originated. Perhaps it reflects the fact that some varieties are too sour to eat right off the tree, although nearly all crabapples are delicious when cooked.

Crabapple Jelly

Use this jelly in yogurt with nuts for breakfast or as a glaze for roasted game or poultry.

Pick a sweet-tart variety of crabapple as it approaches peak ripeness, but include some underripe crabapples for more pectin.

Yield depends on the amount of crabapples picked. Two extra-large mixing bowls of fruit, about 15 to 18 pounds, yields 12 to 16 half-pints.

Rinse the crabapples in batches, leaving plenty of stems. Halve the fruit, place in a heavy enameled pot, and add enough water to cover. Bring to a boil and cook until fruit is soft and the liquid is lightly colored, 5 to 10 minutes. Remove from heat and strain through a cheesecloth-lined sieve into a clean bowl. Do not squeeze or press the pulp, as this clouds the jelly. Let the final batches sit overnight so all the juice can drip through.

The next day, wash and scald canning jars, new lids, bands, and utensils, including a wide-mouth funnel. Measure the juice, up to 8 cups per batch. Bring juice to a rapid boil in a large enameled pot for 5 minutes, removing any froth that forms; at the same time prepare a water bath in a separate kettle for sealing the jars.

Add ¾ to 1 cup of sugar for each cup of juice. Dissolve sugar in the boiling juice, and continue to boil until the mixture reaches the jelling point. Test for this by pouring a small quantity of the mixture off the side of a wide cooking spoon; when it slows and forms a sheet rather than individual drops, the jelly is ready, usually about 15 minutes.

Pour carefully into jars, leaving ¼ to ½ inch headroom, gently cover with lids and bands, and seal in a boiling hot water bath for 20 minutes.

The hardy crabapple variety called Rescue grows as far north as Alberta, Canada, where this specimen produces abundant yellow-green fruit. Photo courtesy of Linda Pierson, Wardlow, Alberta.

Crabapple fruit, it is true, has a tartness that may not be to everyone's liking. But then, I'm spoiled by having a generous neighbor with two heavily bearing crabapple trees in her front yard. Neither of us knows what variety they are, but the fruit, when it ripens, turns a beautiful pink-tinged gold. The taste is like candy, a perfect balance of sweet and tart . . . and juicy. From catalog descriptions we have narrowed them down to the popular Callaway Crab or possibly a Siberian or native American sweet crabapple.

My neighbor also has two delightful young daughters, and every year at hurricane season—usually the first or second week of

September—the three of us spend an hour in the trees picking fruit (nice to know the trees have never been sprayed with toxic chemicals).

Over the next day or so I make jelly and leave a few jars on their doorstep as thanks. I say hurricane season because, living in the mountains of western Carolina, we often feel severe effects of hurricanes hundreds of miles away. Just as the storm clouds begin to mass and warnings come over the radio, I remember that the crabapples will be just right and must be saved from damage. I treasure our warm, portentous afternoon forays.

Crabapples come in many varieties. Commonly on offer are Transcendent, Callaway Crab, Dolgo, Kerr, Hyslop, and Young America. Check with supply houses to see what new cultivars are available, and don't be afraid to call an Agricultural Extension office for specific information about the fruit characteristics.

LANDSCAPE HIGHLIGHTS
- Spring blossoms
- Winter wildlife food source

EDIBLE HIGHLIGHTS
- Fruit preserved as jelly
- Added fresh to apple dishes for flavor
- Canned as juice, alone or mixed with other fruit juices like apple, grape, pear, or cherry

WHERE IT GROWS BEST
- Zones 2–7, to -40°F
- In full sun
- In a place with cold winters
- In moist but well-drained soil

HOW TO GROW IT
- As a garden focal point for spring blossoms
- For harvest after the first frost
- With little pruning or pest control needed

- Near contrasting early spring bulbs
- With birdbath nearby

VARIETIES TO TRY
Crabapples are naturally small, growing from six feet to about thirty feet at most. For best eating try Callaway Crab, Dolgo crab, or the Kerr apple-crabapple hybrid.

Peach

Only fools or optimists grow peaches.
The tree is temperamental: it falls prey to a wider variety of bugs and diseases than most fruit trees, and it needs careful monitoring and treatment. It prefers a moderate winter climate without late spring freezes, and light, well-drained loam rather than heavier garden soil. It requires more pruning—and more skillful pruning—than many other orchard

Dripping with fruit, a well-established peach tree may produce bushels a season. Peaches grow quickly, providing welcome shade within a few years. Photo by Joanne Firth, courtesy of the California Tree Fruit Agreement.

fruits; at least one grower has written that the fast-growing peach "lives by the knife." The peach has a short life span of only fifteen or twenty years.

And yet . . . there's the beautiful, open, vase-like shape of the tree, like a hand raised in supplication, and sprays of pink blossoms in spring, sometimes with hints of yellow or orange like the fruit itself.

Mmmm, the fruit: when plucked ripe from the tree there's nothing to compare. Like something alive, the peach from an edible landscape is warm to the touch, a little fuzzy. Juicy, filled with its own satisfying syrup. As good as a kiss.

A healthy peach tree of bearing age produces bushels of fruit a year. Peaches are nearly as good in their many cooked, baked, or preserved forms as they are fresh. Pie, cobbler, ice cream, chutney, anything. This fruit's combination of taste and texture is one of life's great pleasures.

Peaches managed for long-distance shipping to grocery stores nationwide can never duplicate that experience, because the secret of a tree-ripened peach is the complex development of natural sugars over time.

There's a hopeful quirkiness to peach trees. Despite their many frailties they can survive and flourish in surprising places, and, in fact, they grow in most of the United States, having migrated over centuries from China through Europe to the colonies. Take the case of my gardening friend Marianne's mysterious "mountain peach." Marianne and her husband live on a windswept mountainside near Boone, North Carolina, at four thousand feet elevation. Winters can be intensely cold, with damaging ice and snow. But there in the front yard stands a perfectly formed peach tree, growing more luscious by the year.

The tree blooms every spring, and most summers Marianne harvests huge quantities of fruit, which she makes into preserves.

"How did you get this thing to grow up here, let alone bear fruit?" I once asked. The answer made me laugh. The tree was a volunteer, probably from a pit thrown onto the compost heap, she said. It gets no special attention and has remained disease free for twenty years now.

"Windswept" may be the clue. A peach tree needs good air

Kissed by the sun, a peach on the tree grows more flavorful as natural sugars develop. Photo courtesy of The California Fruit Tree Agreement.

Peaches and Cream Pops

Makes 4 Servings

½ cup peeled, chopped peaches
⅓ cup peeled, pureed peaches
⅔ cup vanilla yogurt

Lightly swirl all ingredients together in a small bowl. Spoon into 4 Popsicle molds and insert handle. Freeze for at least 4 hours.

*For extra-sweet pops, add 1 to 2 tablespoons of honey to yogurt before swirling.

Recipe courtesy of the California Tree Fruit Agreement.

Gran'Pappy's Peach Leather

2½ cups mashed ripe peach pulp
½ cup sugar, plus sugar for sprinkling

Combine pulp and sugar in heavy skillet. Cook and stir until thickened. Spread out in a thin layer on a greased baking sheet; cover with gauze, and put in hot sun to dry for 3 days, bringing it inside at night. When leather pulls away from the pan, it is done. Place on a board sprinkled with sugar, and sprinkle sugar on top. Roll out as thin as a spatula, then cut into strips 1⅛ inches wide. Cut small wafers and roll up. Sprinkle again with sugar, then store in a box with a tight lid.

Recipe reprinted with permission from Southern Appalachian Mountain Cookin': Authentic Ol' Mountain Family Recipes, ©2004, APS, Inc.

Easy to make in volume, Peaches and Cream Pops provide a nutritious snack right out of the freezer. Photo by Joanne Firth, courtesy of the California Tree Fruit Agreement.

circulation, both around and within its limb structure; breezes drive away frost and can also keep the branches and leaves dry and less susceptible to disease.

Similarly, peach trees may do well near a lake or pond that can lessen the likelihood of freeze damage. Planted thus, a peach tree never fails to create landscape drama.

LANDSCAPE HIGHLIGHTS

- Spring blossoms
- Summer harvest and shade
- Fall leaf color

EDIBLE HIGHLIGHTS

- Fresh fruit from the tree
- Canned in syrup
- Dehydrated as "leather"
- Frozen in sections

WHERE IT GROWS BEST

- In zones with moderate winter temperatures, some sub-freezing weather but no late freezes
- In light or sandy soil that drains quickly
- On sloping ground to shed frost
- With specific local characteristics (see Resources section for Agricultural Extension information)

HOW TO GROW IT

- With early spring planting
- With irrigation in dry weather
- With weed-free soil around the trunk
- For quick shade in yards of any size, within three years
- Near lawn furniture for an inviting garden "room"

SPECIAL CARE FOR PEACHES

To produce the best fruit, peach trees require substantial pruning—as much as thirty percent of the wood—each year after the tree is established. When planting new trees, prune to three short limbs to produce an "open center" or vase shape. As the tree matures, continue to remove crossing limbs, suckers, and much growth on main limbs. Pruning keeps the tree structure short and open and allows good air circulation, crucial to minimizing disease and to encouraging flower buds at a convenient height. See http://wilkes.ces.ncsu.edu/files/library/97/How%20to%20Prune%20Peach%20Trees-4.pdf.

Peaches are susceptible to various pests and diseases. For help choosing organic solutions, see Resources section, and stick to any recommended spraying schedule. Disease-resistant varieties are under development.

Fruit thinning may be necessary for full-size fruit and to prevent limbs breaking. To thin fruit, simply pinch off a proportion of flowers or tiny developing fruit, or shake tree vigorously when fruit is young. Remaining fruit should be 6–8 inches apart, or not more than 500 peaches when tree is grown.

Pear

First grow a pear tree.

When I imagine my favorite pear recipe—a weeks-long saga that involves pickling pears in spiced syrup and using them for an olive oil–based torte—that's how I begin.

First, grow a pear tree. It's the ultimate test of patience, for that part alone can take years. That pear trees bear fruit at all is something of a miracle, as pollination may take place over the course of just a few hours each year and several variables must align precisely to produce viable fruit.

Fortunately, I started my twenty-year love affair with fresh

Photo by Debby Morse from madeater.blogspot.com.

pears by finding two mature pear trees on a vacant lot near my children's elementary school.

The kids and I looked at those pears for years, wondering if we should pick some. Then one evening we packed up a ladder and some paper grocery bags and did it. We waded through high grass and sticker bushes for our reward: hundreds of fat green pears, too hard to eat right away but excellent for ripening at home and for those spiced pickles. The kids liked being encouraged to climb trees higher and higher, to reach for the choicest ones.

Human beings have been eating pears since the Stone Age. Pears figured in the cuisine—and the drinking life—of ancient Greece and Rome, and they became part of the nutritional culture of Western Europe before crossing the Atlantic. In Old World folklore, planting a pear tree was a living good-luck charm, especially to welcome the birth of a daughter.

Pickled, baked, poached, thinly sliced with cheese or in a salad, crushed and made into cider or wine—pears have the feel of antiquity. In long-ago France, particularly, pear culture took hold in the favorable soil and climate, and many pear varieties have lovely French names: Beurre d'Amanlis, Doyenne du Comice, Jargonelle, Bellissime d'Hiver, Conseiller de la Cour, and others.

The grainy texture and nectar-like juice of pears are unmistakable; relatively high levels of vitamin C and potassium and very high fiber content make them a valuable source of nourishment. Dried in slices, pears keep well through the year.

In the edible landscape, pears usher in spring with their delicate white blossoms, which attract insects and make the air come alive for the frenzied pollination period. And because the pear tree has such supple wood, it has long been used for training onto walls in the espalier form; the practice enables gardeners to give the tree extra warmth and shelter in cold climates.

Pears are fussy about cold and fertilizer and mustn't have too much of either. Too-rich soil encourages excess vegetation rather than fruiting, but soil must be deeply structured for the long roots.

When planting pear trees in the edible landscape, keep in mind that each variety is self-sterile; there must be at least two varieties near each other for pollination. And not just any two: different pears can be early, midseason, or late bearing, so it's best to choose pairs that are compatible. Newer dwarf stocks are a boon to the

Pear Chutney

3 pounds pears, peeled and chopped

2½ cups vinegar

2 cups brown sugar

1½ teaspoons grated ginger

1 teaspoon ground allspice

1½ teaspoons salt

1 medium green bell pepper, finely chopped

1 medium onion, finely chopped

½ cup golden raisins

2 teaspoons grated lemon zest

3 tablespoons fresh lemon juice

Place the pears in the vinegar in a nonreactive metal saucepan. Stir in the sugar and spices, and bring to a boil. Add all other ingredients and simmer until thick, about 1 hour.

Pack into 3 sterilized pint canning jars with new, scalded bands and new lids. Leave ½ inch head space. Quickly invert the jars, leaving them upturned for five minutes. When turned right side up, they should seal.

Pears grow in espalier form near the kitchen garden of Oatlands Historic House and Gardens in Leesburg, Virginia. Photo by Carla Johnston for Oatlands Historic House and Gardens.

home gardener, as the trees are easier to maintain and require less space.

Pears are highly unusual in needing to be picked before they are ripe. That's because they ripen from the inside out, and by the time the outer layer is ready, the inside has turned to mush. To test for readiness, hold each ripening pear in your cupped palm and turn the hand upward. If the stem separates easily from the tree, it's time.

LANDSCAPE HIGHLIGHTS
- Spring blossoms
- Espaliered for year-round interest on wall

EDIBLE HIGHLIGHTS
- Fruit ripened off the tree
- Pressed for fermentation
- Canned whole in spiced syrup
- Poached or baked as dessert
- Dehydrated for winter snacking

WHERE IT GROWS BEST
- In full or partial sun, in a cool or cold climate
- In soil that's not too rich, to discourage excess leaf growth at the expense of fruit
- In generally dry garden conditions to discourage blight, but with occasional watering
- On dwarf rootstock for ease of care and harvest

HOW TO GROW IT
- With other pear varieties for cross-pollination
- Without much pruning
- With soil weeded around trees to discourage rodents
- With excess fruit thinned to prevent limbs breaking
- Against a brick wall, pruned and trained on wires for symmetrical shape, old-world style
- In moderate climates in pairs scattered in a large yard

CROSS-POLLINATION TIPS
Pears are self-sterile, that is, they cannot become fertilized and bear fruit without another variety nearby, preferably one that blooms and bears fruit around the same time in the season.

The reliable Bartlett pear, the Rousselet of Stuttgart, and Clapp's Favorite all ripen in late August. Seckel pear, Beurre D'Anjou, Orcas, and Bosc all ripen in September. Seckel and Bartlett are a non-fertilizing European pear combination. Asian pears also cross-pollinate; try Hosui with Chojuro and Shinseiki.

See Resources section for Agricultural Extension information about best local characteristics.

Plum

My memories of the plums in my family's backyard are fifty years old but bright as sunshine. It was full summer in Fresno, California, and a band of half-grown boys—they looked so menacing but were probably twelve—streamed into the yard with baseball bats and headed right to a plum tree. I watched from the safety of the house, a scared five- or six-year-old.

Photo courtesy of the California Tree Fruit Agreement.

We had two plum trees, one of them with immense dark-purple fruits colored red on the inside: juicy and delicious. The other tree was smaller, with small, light-colored plums; they weren't as sweet, and as far as we kids were concerned, that tree was only good for climbing.

Those big boys grabbed handfuls of the overripe fruit that had fallen to the ground, and they hit the lower branches with their bats for more. They tossed a few of the plums into the air and hit them like baseballs. Splat! The skins burst and pulp and juice went flying. The boys laughed hard, grabbed their plum booty, and fled to the middle of our otherwise quiet street to continue their game of plum baseball. The pavement was a mess afterward.

Ah, how sweet those days of careless excess. If I had those two plum trees today, of course, I'm sure I would be baking, cooking, drying, and canning the fruit to capture some of that summer-flavored goodness for the rest of the year. The encouraging news is there's no reason, with time, that I can't have homegrown plums again. There are already two young trees started in my edible landscape in western North Carolina.

Plums have been called the "most various" kind of fruit tree in America. With two main types of plum—European and Japanese—and many hybrids of each, there's a plum tree for every climate and soil type (so contact your local Agricultural Extension office). A third strain consists of the American native plum species; according to some classification systems, the Damson is a separate plum type. Some of the many fruiting plum varieties have purple-tinged leaves, and there's a non-fruiting ornamental "purple-leaf" variety with striking dark leaves.

The European plums, which include the tart Damsons as well as high-sugar prune plums for drying, are popular for eating fresh, cooking, or canning; Japanese plums are known for eating fresh. American natives produce edible fruit that can be made into

Hiding in the shade, plums ripen gradually to their full sugary goodness in the edible landscape. Photo courtesy of the California Tree Fruit Agreement.

Rose Water Plum Compote

5 pounds plums
1/3 cup fresh lemon juice
1 pound sugar (fine-grain organic cane sugar)
3 tablespoons rose water

Have a big bowl ready. Pit and chop the plums into small 1/2-inch pieces. As you chop, place the chopped plums in the bowl and toss with a drizzle of the lemon juice every once in a while. When all the plums have been chopped, gently toss them with any remaining lemon juice and the sugar. Stir in the rose water. If possible, let the mixture sit for twenty minutes or so.

In a large, wide, thick-bottomed pot, bring the plum mixture to a boil over medium heat. Stir regularly, scraping the bottom of the pot to make sure the fruit doesn't burn. Adjust the heat if needed and cook at a lazy boil for about 20 to 25 minutes, skimming off any foam that develops. Be mindful of the texture of the fruit; you don't want to overcook (or over-stir) the fruit to the point that it breaks down and goes to mush.

Remove from heat and spoon the compote into individual jars. Refrigerate until ready to use. It will keep for about a week like this. Makes about eight half-pint jars.

Recipe courtesy of Heidi Swanson / 101cookbooks.com.

Crops can be huge as plum trees come into their bearing years. That's why a good recipe for preserves is worth keeping close at hand. Photo courtesy of Heidi Swanson, www.101cookbooks.com.

preserves, and with their lower, shrubby habit, they can add needed screening in the landscape.

In general, plum trees like dry heat. They require some pruning, of course, and if they have proper pollination (in some cases cross-pollination) and fertilizer, they can bear hundreds of pounds of fruit a year over a long harvest. Their beautiful pale pink or white blossoms evenly spaced along twisting branches are a symbol of springtime perfection.

Meaty and nutritious, plums lend themselves to all kinds of culinary uses: baked into breads and cakes, roasted with meats, and made into jams, chutneys, wines, cordials, and dried fruit leathers. Prunes are simply dried plums and have a wide range of uses on their own.

LANDSCAPE HIGHLIGHTS
- Spring blossoms
- Summer harvest

EDIBLE HIGHLIGHTS
- Fresh fruit from the tree
- Dehydrated as prunes
- Canned as jam or compote

WHERE IT GROWS BEST
- In zones with warm or hot summers but cold winters (to -30 degrees F, Zone 4, depending on variety)
- In full or half-day sun
- In well-drained soil, not too rich
- Spaced at least twenty feet apart

HOW TO GROW IT
- With only light pruning to allow light and air into framework
- With planting in fall and pruning in spring
- With fruit thinning to prevent overbearing and damage to trees
- With other varieties for cross-pollination
- Not best as centerpiece of garden, but mixed into border areas for spring color

Quince

On a continuum of the pome fruits—apple, pear, and quince—quince is considered the hardest because it has the highest concentration of "stone cells," which give quinces their especially granular, almost gritty, skin and tough fruit. Quinces may also be the most beautiful of the pome fruits, with twisting branches, a compact shape that needs little care, and supremely attractive creamy pink blossoms in early spring.

Quince blossoms daub the spring landscape with creamy pink blooms. The fruit is tough but is flavorful in preserves and sauces when cooked. Photo by Nan K. Chase.

"A quince tree is beautiful in flower, leaf, and fruit, and is an ornament on any lawn," wrote one orchardsman. "Every owner of a fruit garden should have two or three quinces."

Some biblical scholars contend that the apple in the Garden of Eden was really a quince. Indeed the quince was familiar through-out Greek mythology and made an appearance in Roman cook-books—stewed with honey—and in cosmetics (hair dye) and cough medicines of the day.

The quince brings four seasons of enjoyment to the edible land-scape and some interesting possibilities in the kitchen.

Spring flowers begin the cycle, followed by lush foliage in sum-mer, slowly ripening fruit in fall and through the first frosts, and, finally, winter interest as snow settles onto the tangled limbs.

Topping out at about twenty-four feet, the self-fertile quince can also be pruned to good effect. Some varieties, including the lovely contorted quince, grow considerably lower.

Horticulturalists indicate that the quince grows in exactly the same places the apple grows and so doesn't do well in the very hot-test regions of the South and West. Quinces have the same need as apples for good air circulation around and through the branches, and for adequate drainage.

That has certainly been the case in my own yard. In years when a late frost knocks out the apple blossoms, my small quince bush at the edge of the yard is hard-hit too. But when the apples bud out and set fruit, so does the quince—and that's magical. The rosy-green young fruits look like gourds as they ripen over the long growing season and take on their yellow burnish.

Because of complications in plant nomenclature, be sure to inves-tigate quinces of the genus *Cydonia* and flowering quinces of the genus *Chaenomeles*, both of which bear fruit.

Though the quince fruit is tough, it has a rich fragrance and strong, distinctive flavor as compensation. There are many varieties of quince, with fruit of varying degrees of sweetness; few of them can be eaten out of hand but rather are used for cooking: juice, jelly, marmalade, sauces, baked goods, and more.

Some cooks insist on a few slices of quince in apple pies and bits of quince in applesauce. One tantalizing recipe for quince sauce contains cloves, port, honey, white wine, grape juice, and lemon

Membrillo (Quince Paste)

5 pounds quinces, skin left on, quartered and cored
2¼ cups water
Juice of 1 lemon
Sugar
1 cinnamon stick
Baking paper, not waxed paper, and sufficient butter or
　　other shortening to coat

Bring quinces, water, and lemon juice to a boil, and then reduce heat. Simmer with the lid on for 45 minutes. Use a hand blender to puree the fruit and water.

Measure the puree and add to a clean pan along with an equal weight of sugar and the cinnamon stick. Gently heat the paste over a low heat, stirring frequently.

After 30 to 45 minutes the paste should be thickening. Keep a closer eye on the paste at this point, stirring continually.

Once the paste has become thick enough to stand a spoon in and is a deep orange color, remove the pan from the heat.

Tip mixture into a shallow baking tray or ovenproof dish lined with greased baking paper. Keep in a warm place (near radiator or in very slow oven) for 12 hours.

Your paste is now ready! Store in foil in an airtight container for up to a year.

Recipe courtesy of A Wee Bit of Cooking: A Scottish Food Blog, http://teach77. wordpress.com/.

juice, but no added sugar; another calls for pheasant "roasted with quinces and ginger wine."

Consider quince wine, quince leather, candied or crystallized quince, and a loaf-shaped quince paste, called "membrillo" in some parts, which is a favorite dish in Europe, Latin America, and the Middle East, especially when served with white cheese. It was membrillo that I loved to eat in Bogotá, Colombia, during a college semester there. Membrillo melts in the mouth, sweet and grainy.

Photo © iStockPhoto/Lucylui.

LANDSCAPE HIGHLIGHTS

- Spring blossoms
- Winter interest with snow

EDIBLE HIGHLIGHTS

- Cooked as paste
- Dehydrated as "leather"
- Canned as sauce or jelly
- Baked into apple recipes
- Candied or crystallized

WHERE IT GROWS BEST

- In any climate where apples grow, depending on variety (cold winters, warm summers)
- In any but very wet soil
- In full or half-day sun
- With trunk free from weeds or vines

HOW TO GROW IT

- As a large shrub from four to twenty feet tall
- As a disease- and pest-free fruiting plant
- Massed as a hedge, or singly as specimens
- Along a property line as a productive natural fence
- In front of ornamental grasses for textural contrast
- With light pruning to eliminate crossing branches

Nuts & Berries

Grand, majestic, and noble. Nut trees add so much to an edible landscape—if you have the space and the proper climate—and so much to a nutritious diet.

"Steeped in holy lore," as the folk wine expert M. A. Jagendorf once wrote, many nut trees had symbolic—and often conflicting—roles in history; in ancient Athens and Rome walnut trees stood for "fertility, abundance, and regeneration" and were showered on newlyweds. In other places nut trees were equated with poison and devilish deeds. Walnut shells appeared in some tales as magical boats, and in others, walnuts could ward off epilepsy, lightning, and witches.

Now, across large portions of North America, nut trees are treasured for their fine wood, their restful shade and fine profiles, their flavorful fruit, and in some cases, their flowers. Foods cooked with nuts are among our favorites: roasted nuts for snacking and salads, nut accompaniments for game and poultry, nut desserts with chocolate and cream, nut spreads and butters, nut breads and waffles and muffins. There are even recipes for wines made from the leaves of nut trees to capture their subtlest characteristics.

Many nut trees are related to each other and to other fruiting trees. The pecan and the hickory are kin, as are almonds and peaches. And, like favorite orchard fruits, the various nut species have specific requirements for heat, humidity, soil, and pollination. Nut trees are fairly long lived and in general require a long growing period to produce edible nuts, and thus need mild winters without danger of late frosts that can destroy tender blossoms and budding fruit.

The large size of some nut trees is part of their value in the

Walnut trees enhance the edible landscape in fall, when their drooping boughs turn to gold. The nuts are borne in tough husks that must be broken away. Photo by Lisa Wheeler Milton.

edible landscape. They provide stunning year-round focus, but it is their shade in summer that matters most.

In very hot parts of the country—the Deep South and California's Central Valley—the shade takes on a lifesaving quality from the elements, and it indicates the presence of human habitation on the flat and sometimes bleak horizon. But that means the largest nut trees don't belong in a city garden or even necessarily in the suburbs, but rather on a wide-open country homestead. The root systems can extend far beyond the spread of the branches, and so trees mustn't be crowded.

Flowers on nut trees assume marvelous and varied forms: the simple and delicate pink-white blooms of the almond, the complex and odoriferous flowers of chestnuts high overhead, the graceful catkins of walnut and hazelnut.

Alas, nut trees also have inconvenient parts (chestnuts drop their prickly burrs, almonds their hulls, walnuts their tough husks) that must be picked up to keep the yard neat and bare feet uninjured.

The reward of edible nuts is incalculable, however. Nuts are elemental and densely packed with the requirements of health; in fact, their nutritional value is often figured as equivalent to that of meat. Some nut "meats," as the inner nut fruits are called, have compounds that fight heart disease and diabetes, and they are rich in vitamins, minerals, and beneficial fats.

Begin today with nut trees, as long as you have the space, and grow old with them in health beneath their boughs.

Not all berry bushes are attractive in the landscape, no matter how delicious their fruit. Blackberries and raspberries—not so nice. Currants fade into the background except when their berries shine through, and they are illegal to grow in some states because of disease risks to commercially valuable plants; gooseberries have the same problem. Strawberries: wonderful fruit but little landscape value.

But the highbush blueberry is another matter. It offers four seasons of beauty: winter, spring, summer, and fall. And its berries are among the most healthful and delicious of all homegrown foods.

Almond

With fragrant, ruby-throated pink or white blossoms that signal the earliest arrival of spring, the almond has lived alongside people since the dawn of civilization.

Thousands of years ago the almond tree, a member of the rose family and close relative to the peach, came under cultivation and then spread from the arid highlands of Asia to the Mediterranean basin, marking what eventually would be called the Silk Road. The

A rare treat, green almonds are eaten when the kernels are still jelly-like. Some cooks blanch these inner seeds, fry them in olive oil, and then salt them lightly. Photo courtesy of Amy Glaze, Paris, France.

tree took hold through the Middle East and the Greek world and into the warmer sections of Europe and North Africa.

Franciscan brothers from Spain took almonds to their mission compounds in California in the 1700s, and it was there, after pioneering East Coast efforts to grow them failed, that the trees eventually took hold farther inland from the Pacific Coast. Today, virtually all almond production for United States consumption and most of the worldwide market takes place in California.

Almond Biscotti

3 large eggs
Grated peel of 2 oranges
1 teaspoon vanilla
1/2 teaspoon almond extract
2 cups flour
1 cup sugar
1 teaspoon baking soda
1/4 teaspoon salt
3/4 cup toasted whole natural almonds

Heat oven to 300 degrees F. Coat a large baking sheet with vegetable cooking spray or cover with baking parchment. In bowl, whisk eggs, orange peel, vanilla, and almond extract. In large bowl, combine flour, sugar, baking soda, and salt. Add egg mixture; mix just until blended. Mix in almonds. Divide dough in half.

Form each half into a log measuring about 12 inches long, 1 1/2 inches wide, and 1/2 inch thick. Bake in the center of the oven, about 50 minutes, until golden. Remove to a cooling rack for 5 minutes. Reduce oven heat to 275 degrees F. Place logs on a cutting board and, with a serrated knife, slice on the diagonal 1/2 inch thick. Lay slices flat on baking sheets, spacing slightly apart. Return to oven until dry and lightly toasted, 20 to 25 minutes, turning once. Place on racks to cool completely. Store in an airtight container.

Makes about 3 1/2 dozen.

Recipe courtesy of 2008 Almond Board of California.

It's not that the almond tree won't grow anywhere else, but its blossoming period a month before even the peach means that to bear fruit reliably it must live where late frosts don't occur.

Handsome and upright in form, almond trees grow to a manageable twenty-five feet and make fine specimen plants in the edible landscape; the life span is generally twenty to twenty-five years. They are often pruned to accentuate their naturally interesting gnarled limbs and to give the garden a touch of antiquity.

Photo © iStockPhoto/Levente Varga (levifoto).

LANDSCAPE HIGHLIGHTS

- Spring blossoms

EDIBLE HIGHLIGHTS

- Air-dried for snacks or baking
- Ground for almond paste or butter
- Nut kernels blanched in an unripe state, then pan-fried as a snack

WHERE IT GROWS BEST

- In moderate winter cold without any late frost, similar to climate for peaches but blooming one month earlier
- In full or half-day sun
- Away from wet soil, preferring sandy or well-worked conditions

HOW TO GROW IT

- With other almond varieties for cross-pollination (Prima, Bounty, Nikita's Pride, and Seaside all bloom late)
- With light fertilizing
- With early pruning to form open limb structure
- With dropped nuts picked up to prevent disease in trees
- Near a fence or other garden architectural feature for long-range interest
- With seating nearby for summer shade
- In a corner of a small garden for a focal point

TO HARVEST ALMONDS

The outer pulpy hull splits open in fall as nuts ripen. Spread sheets on the ground, shake or knock nuts off, then let dry in shade. Kernels keep well inside their dry brown shell.

Closely related to peaches, almond trees produce fruits of similar structure and appearance, at least as the fuzzy husks first develop. Photo by Henry Firus of Flagstaffotos, Australia.

Almond trees need cross-pollination with other varieties that bloom at the same time; California growers typically plant three kinds of trees close together. If you keep bees, almonds should do particularly well.

My family moved to a small house in Fresno, California, when I was three years old. Among all the other marvelous fruit trees in the backyard was an almond tree of bearing age; who knows where its partner—its pollinator—lived, but it must have been nearby. How lucky we were to be able to pick almonds off the tree, off the ground, and eat them as playtime snacks. The flavor was mysterious, the texture almost milky.

The almond that we love to eat sits inside a light brown, pitted shell, which, in turn, ripens within a protective husk. The almond husk and the developing young peach fruit look almost identical during the early stages.

Almond trees bloom in February and March and then set fruits that ripen into heavy clusters through May and June. In July and August the hulls split open, but the nuts remain on the tree until they are knocked off mechanically during the harvest, which lasts as late as October. Almonds then must be air-dried, usually on sheets laid on the ground, for eight or ten days before they are ready for processing, use, and storage. Properly handled, almonds can retain their nutritional value and flavor for a year.

Blueberry

Biggest "wow" factor? That would be the highbush blueberry, which has great value in the landscape throughout the year, plus abundant fruit of outstanding flavor and top nutritional content.

The list of the blueberry bush's admirable qualities goes on and on: it is insect-resistant and extremely cold hardy, has a compact habit that makes it perfect in the small garden, doesn't require much

Perfect in a rock garden or terraced yard, blueberry bushes turn blazing scarlet in fall and create drama alongside evergreens. Photo by Lonnie Webster.

weeding or pruning, grows best with simple organic methods, and produces the natural food highest in health-promoting antioxidants.

The only real downside to using blueberries in the edible landscape is that the fruit is irresistible to birds, and so nets must be erected every year to protect the harvest.

Blueberries are members of the heath family, which includes azaleas and rhododendrons, mountain laurels, cranberries, and huckleberries. If you understand the conditions in which all those plants

Nan's Blueberry Jam

The standard proportion for blueberry jam is four parts cleaned fruit (with a little water) to three parts sugar; usually that means 3 cups of sugar to 4 cups of fruit.

4 to 8 cups blueberries, cleaned
(include some under-ripe berries for pectin)
3 cups sugar for each 4 cups fruit
1 apple per batch, cored and cut into small pieces with skin on, for pectin

Wash and scald canning jars, new lids, bands, and utensils (including wide-mouth funnel and canning tongs).

Working them in batches, rinse the berries and pick out stems, leaves, and imperfect fruit, and place along with apple in a heavy enameled pot with enough water to cover. Bring to a boil and cook until fruit is soft and liquid runs freely; then mash the fruit.

Dissolve the sugar in the boiling juice and continue to boil until the mixture reaches the jelling point. Test for this by pouring a small quantity of the mixture off the side of a wide cooking spoon; when it slows and forms a sheet rather than individual drops, usually 15 to 20 minutes, jam is ready. Skim any froth that develops.

Pour carefully into jars using the wide-mouth funnel, leaving 1/4 to 1/2 inch headroom; cover gently with lids and bands and seal in a boiling hot water bath.

grow, you know how blueberries should best be used.

The heath family, including blueberries, must have the light, rich leaf litter and compost of the forest floor, or at least the high organic content that accompanies natural decomposition. And the soil must be acid, or corrected to a pH around 5.0.

The various kinds of blueberries have shallow roots that spread near the top layer of soil; blueberries do best without weeding but with the occasional addition of humus and organic fertilizers. And as they would in their natural setting at the edge of a forest, blueberries require a good amount of moisture and excellent drainage.

For all those reasons, highbush blueberries look exceptionally handsome in rock gardens or mixed into steep, rocky, or terraced terrain.

I love the waxy blossoms in spring, which are at once modest—small and creamy white—and spectacular: clustered, downward facing, and as graceful as alabaster vases.

In summer the blueberry bushes fill out and the ripening berries take center stage. Nets must go up just after fruit sets, before the fruit gets too big and is easily knocked off. It only took me one minute—on the morning that I discovered birds had eaten an entire year's imminent harvest at dawn, while I slept—to decide that nets and cages were worth the effort.

Once harvest is finished in late summer, the nets come down so we can enjoy the fall color. Blueberry leaves turn a deep coppery red and stay late on the bushes. Moistened with autumn rain, they are melancholy and brilliant.

Even in winter there's beauty, whenever ice coats the graceful branches.

There's a second main type of blueberry, the lowbush blueberry. This plant grows almost exclusively in cold, wet northern Michigan and northern New England, and also through the Southern Appalachians. The lowbush blueberry produces loads of intensely flavorful fruit, but because it must grow in extensive thickets—ideally on burned-over wasteland—it is cultivated mostly as a commercial crop.

Hybrids of highbush and lowbush blueberries are constantly under development, so keep an eye on new offerings. Blueberries require cross-pollination from two or more varieties; plant in volume.

LANDSCAPE
HIGHLIGHTS
• Spring blossoms
• Summer harvest
• Fall leaf color
• Winter interest

EDIBLE HIGHLIGHTS
• Fresh fruit from the bush
• Canned as jam or syrup
• Frozen for year-round use
• Dehydrated as "raisins"

WHERE IT GROWS BEST
• In acidic soil, pH 5 to 5.6

• In full sun or dappled shade
• In cold climates (hardy to -45 degrees F, depending on variety)
• Spaced four to six feet apart for fruit production

HOW TO GROW IT
• With cross-pollination for fruit production (see Resources section for Agricultural Extension information on local recommendations)
• With light applications of compost or an acidic mulch

• With minimal weeding that would disturb shallow roots
• With light pruning every few years to remove older branches
• With bird netting or wire cages to protect fruit (see Bird Netting, page 19)
• As a pest-free shrub
• In rock gardens
• In steep, terraced gardens
• Next to evergreen trees or bushes for fall contrast

Chestnut

Once upon a time a vast forest covered the eastern part of what became the United States. From Maine to Michigan to Georgia, a quarter or more of these ancient trees were American chestnuts, *Castanea dentata*.

The American chestnut tree, "Redwood of the East," grew to immense proportions: more than one hundred feet tall and ten feet across, straight and solid, with deeply furrowed

The chestnut tree's prickly burrs have a rough beauty all their own. Inside there's treasure, if you can stay ahead of hungry squirrels. Photo courtesy of Forestfarm/R. Prag.

bark. The chestnut tree provided prodigious quantities of rot-resistant wood and delicious nuts, plus midsummer shade and impressive blooms.

Millions of people relied on chestnuts for their livelihood and for food; country people fattened their livestock on chestnuts and cooked chestnuts for their own supper, and they sold the surplus by trainloads. "Chestnuts roasting on an open fire" were part of the American scene for generations.

Then, in 1904, chestnut blight came to this country and, within forty years, virtually all of the trees were gone. Several billion trees are thought to have died outright; others survived as rootstock but had their new shoots above ground quickly claimed by "ulcerating cankers." A very few American chestnut trees somehow survived and have formed the basis of subsequent breeding programs. Other native chestnut species, like the dainty chinquapin (or chinkapin), were not affected, nor were chestnut varieties from China, Japan, and Europe.

Today, following decades of intensive hybridizing, chestnut trees are now widely available to enjoy in the edible landscape, and even a blight-resistant American chestnut is getting closer to being reestablished.

Fresh chestnuts are fantastic, buttery and sweet with a light crumbly texture. Roasted, candied, boiled, or made into soup, puree, poultry stuffing, or creamy desserts—chestnuts are always good. They're high in protein and low in saturated fat.

But while they are considered similar in nutritional value to brown rice, they don't keep long without some kind of intervention: refrigeration in perforated plastic bags, freezing, drying, pickling, or other. Chestnuts can be ground into gluten-free flour for baking. Once stabilized, these chestnut by-products can keep for months.

Today, with the American chestnut out of the picture, home gardeners choose their chestnut trees from Chinese, Japanese, or European chestnut varieties or from hybrids that combine various characteristics (check for cross-pollination needs).

The readily available Chinese chestnut, for example, is not as tall as its American cousin (growing only to fifty feet or so) but it has large, sweet nuts and a beautiful rounded crown that makes it a wonderful choice for medium-size gardens. The leaves, long and deeply serrated, are a glossy dark green. Masses of long cream-colored catkins make a bold floral statement in early summer but have a strange odor—worse than old socks.

Chestnut trees are not fussy about soil type, although they need good drainage, and a chestnut makes a good young tree for taming rough hillsides. The trees, once established, come into bearing as young as three or four years of age and then go on bearing for half a century. Yields of one hundred pounds of nuts per tree in a season are possible. The tree can survive temperatures well below zero.

Chocolate Chestnut Filling for Cream Puffs

1 1/3 cups peeled chestnuts, about 20

1 cup milk

1 cup granulated sugar

4 ounces semisweet chocolate

2 tablespoons rum or brandy

1 1/4 cups heavy cream

Cream puffs, frozen or homemade

Confectioners' sugar for dusting or small amount of melted chocolate

In a small saucepan, combine peeled chestnuts, milk, and granulated sugar. Bring to a boil, stirring to dissolve the sugar. Simmer for 30 minutes or until chestnuts are tender. While the chestnuts are simmering, melt the chocolate in a microwave for 30 seconds to 1 minute, or melt in a double boiler.

Puree the cooked chestnuts, milk, chocolate, and rum or brandy in a food processor until smooth. Cool slightly. Whip cream to soft peaks and then fold it gently into the chestnut-chocolate mix. The mixture will be soft, so refrigerate at least 1 hour.

When ready to assemble, cut a third of the top off the cream puffs and pipe or spoon the chocolate-chestnut mixture into cream puffs. Replace tops and dust with confectioners' sugar or drizzle with melted chocolate.

Recipe courtesy of Delmarvelous Chestnuts.

Roast Chestnuts

Roasting chestnuts is easy at home, and they are especially delicious over a fire using a long-handled frying pan.

Start with 1/2 to 1 pound nuts in the shell. Cut a deep X into the flat side of each nut to prevent their exploding. Stovetop: use a deep cast iron skillet and roll nuts frequently as you cook 5 to 10 minutes over medium high heat (no oil). Oven: cook nuts in an ungreased baking pan 30 to 40 minutes at 425 degrees F, stirring several times.

Photo courtesy of The Connecticut Agricultural Experiment Station.

LANDSCAPE HIGHLIGHTS

- Summer shade
- Fall harvest

EDIBLE HIGHLIGHTS

- Nuts steamed or roasted as a snack
- Frozen or refrigerated for year-round use
- Candied or pureed as dessert

WHERE IT GROWS BEST

- In a large yard with ample space
- In slightly acid soil
- In well-drained soil rich in organic material
- In roughly the same temperate regions as the peach

HOW TO GROW IT

- Spaced at least twenty-five feet apart
- With mulch to protect shallow roots
- With nuts picked up promptly to prevent worm infestation
- Without too much fertilizer

HOW TO GET STARTED

In addition to selling seeds and seedlings of the beleaguered American chestnut, The American Chestnut Foundation offers a list of suppliers for hybrid chestnuts and other nut trees and products at www.acf.org/seeds_seedlings.php and linked pages. Not all products can be shipped to every state.

Hazelnut/Filbert

Crack! The sound of a ripe hazelnut being broken open before Thanksgiving dinner is unmistakable. So is the ruddy color of the hard little shell. Hazelnut flavor: that's unmistakable too, sweet and earthy, with a little crunch.

Hazelnut, filbert. They're interchangeable as far as the nut industry is concerned and, botanically speaking, quite close.

The important thing is that the filbert, or hazelnut, grows

Hazelnut flowers appear as delicate hanging clusters, or catkins, that seem to glow from within. Photo ©iStockPhoto/ Robert Redelowski.

as a beautiful shrub or small tree with year-round interest. Pendulous catkins—the blooms—hang like golden chains from the bare branches in late winter. During summer the rounded, many-pleated leaves provide islands of shade as the nuts develop. In fall the leaves glow red and gold.

Some filberts have special landscape value on their own—the contorted filbert, or Harry Lauder's Walking Stick, for instance—and are grown as specimen trees. Others are chosen for screening; filberts rarely grow taller than twenty feet, and some stay much smaller. Because filberts need cross-pollination with other varieties, it's imperative to mix and match anyway.

There are two ways to grow filberts: as individual trees with single, or at most a few, trunks; and as a hedge of medium height. Imagine a garden plant with such versatility.

The natural growing habit features "suckering," or the tendency for the plant to throw up many extra shoots around the main trunk. That's perfect for a hedge configuration; space the plants just four feet apart and let the suckers fill in the spaces. For more intense nut production as well as for ornamental treatment, situate the plants about fifteen feet apart and keep suckers off. Hazelnut trees may need to be netted once nut production begins; squirrels love them.

"Heavy, rich land should be avoided," advises one filbert master. These marvelous nut trees prefer a light, edge-of-the-forest soil with good drainage and not too much nutrient content; the trees

A hazelnut tree holds lots of visual and tactile interest. Photo coutesy of Raintree Nursery.

Sweet & Spicy Hazelnuts

Yield: 3 cups

1 pound shelled hazelnuts (about 3 cups)
1 egg white
1 tablespoon water
1/3 cup sugar
1/4 teaspoon ground cinnamon
1/4 teaspoon ground nutmeg
2 teaspoons kosher salt
1/2 teaspoon cayenne pepper

Preheat oven to 350 degrees F. Spread nuts on a large, rimmed baking sheet and bake 6 to 8 minutes, or until they are lightly roasted and the skin starts to come off.

Remove from the oven and let cool. With a clean, non-fuzzy dish towel, rub the skins off the nuts. Reserve the baking sheet.

Meanwhile, reduce oven heat to 250 degrees F. In a medium bowl, whisk egg white and water until foamy. Add hazelnuts and toss to coat well. Transfer the nuts to a sieve, shake, and then drain for at least 2 minutes. Mix all remaining ingredients in a large bowl. Add drained nuts and toss to coat.

On the baking sheet, spread nuts in a single layer. Bake for 30 minutes. Stir with a spatula, spread the nuts out again, and bake 25 to 30 minutes longer, or until the nuts are dry. Loosen the nuts from the baking sheet and let them cool to room temperature on the sheet. Let the nuts cool completely and become crisp before putting them away. They can be stored for up to one month in an airtight container.

Recipe courtesy of The Hazelnut Council.

Emerging in winter's cold, hazelnut catkins mark the beginning of the reproductive cycle. Once fertilized, they develop into clumps of nuts. Photo ©iStockPhoto/Robert Redelowski.

will grow too much vegetation and not enough fruit if given an overindulgent diet. Likewise, they don't particularly relish a burning sun but like a bit of dappled canopy nearby.

One generality is that filberts thrive where peaches also grow. That is, they like some warmth but can succeed in a colder climate if well sheltered from wind and damp frost.

In the edible landscape, filberts mix well with low-growing wild-flowers and spring bulbs. That's where I have planted three different varieties in my yard. They're still young but look happy, and I'm looking forward to a harvest of the delicious "heart-healthy" nuts in a few years.

LANDSCAPE HIGHLIGHTS
- Winter interest with snow
- Winter-spring catkin blooms
- Summer screening
- Fall leaf color

EDIBLE HIGHLIGHTS
- Nuts shelled for snacks or baking

WHERE IT GROWS BEST
- In a rich, loamy soil
- In dappled shade or at the edge of woods
- In cool climates, withstanding sub-zero temperatures

HOW TO GROW IT
- As specimen shrubs, with suckers removed for nut production, or massed as a hedge
- With other varieties for cross-pollination (try 'Delta' and 'Gamma' varieties, or the contorted form Harry Lauder's Walking Stick)
- As a winter blooming plant

HOW TO HARVEST NUTS
Nut husks fade from green to yellow to brown. Ripe nuts should rattle in their shells. Place in a basin of water; eliminate those that float. Dry the remainder in open air before storing in containers. Keep at moderate temperature.

Pecan

My friend Kinney had the misfortune of growing up in South Carolina's pecan country. At least that's how he saw it from his childish perspective, believing that children everywhere were cursed with a dozen pecan trees in their front yard.

"That's all we did Thanksgiving, pick pecans," he still laments from his current home in pecan-unfriendly western North Carolina. "My knees would be raw. It was cold and nasty. You'd have to climb up the tree first and shake it, and the nuts would hit you on the head. We had thirteen trees, and one time I picked twenty-five grocery bags full.

The wonderful taste and texture make the pecan an American favorite. Photo courtesy of the Georgia Pecan Commission.

"Now, of course, I'd give anything to have those trees back. I do love pecans."

Lots of people love pecans. Their sweet, tender nutmeats, purportedly the tree nut highest in antioxidants, lend themselves to every meal. Roasted pecans—salted, sugared, or spiced—are favorite party fare, and pecan pie is an American standard.

In fact, the "sweet pecan," a member of the walnut family, is a North American native. Early colonists found that the Indians depended on pecan nuts for food and quickly came to appreciate that nutritional value themselves.

Whereas many orchard trees had their origins in Europe or Asia and then migrated to the New World, in the case of the pecan, the flow of traffic went the other way. Today the United States produces most of the world's pecans, but the tree also grows far away.

The pecan, considered the largest and "fastest growing" of the hickories (itself a branch of the walnut family), sprang from the moist, sandy lowlands of the Mississippi and moved westward to Texas. The Latin name, *Carya illinoensis,* refers to the pecan's habitat along the Mississippi basin as far north as today's Illinois. In the Algonquin language the name "pecan" meant "nut requiring a stone to crack." George Washington and Thomas Jefferson both loved pecan trees and planted them.

The golden autumn color of the pecan's many-leaved branches is notable in the edible landscape, and the heavy nut clusters make an impressive decorative statement as the nuts ripen.

Today the pecan grows commercially in more than a dozen southern states and several in the West. Tall and stately, pecan trees thrive and produce nuts only with a frost-free growing season of 180 days, and summer weather that's hot and humid.

The rewards are great: this stately tree can live three hundred years and grow to 150 feet.

Pecans require a large yard—using about seventy feet square—but provide shade for multitudes, in addition to their precious elongated nutmeats.

If you want to plant pecans, be sure to respect their preferred setting: warm, wet, open, and low. Then get ready to enjoy the harvest.

Game Day Pecan Pie

½ cup self-rising flour

1 cup sugar

½ cup butter, melted and slightly cooled

2 eggs, beaten slightly

1 cup chopped pecans

1 (9-ounce) package of chocolate chips

2 tablespoons or more of bourbon (up to 6 tablespoons)

1 (9-inch) pastry pie crust, without top

Whipped cream

Preheat oven to 350 degrees F. Mix flour and sugar in a small bowl. Combine remaining ingredients except pie crust and whipped cream in a large bowl and add the flour-sugar mixture. Pour into prepared pie crust and bake 50 minutes to 1 hour. Let cool before cutting. Serve with whipped cream.

Recipe courtesy of the Carreker family of Georgia.

Nan's Braised Brussels Sprouts

1 cup boiling water or chicken stock

4 to 6 dried shiitake mushrooms

½ pound or more Brussels sprouts

1 tablespoon butter

1 teaspoon sugar

⅓ cup or more coarsely chopped pecans

Dash salt

Put boiling water or stock in a small bowl and soak mushrooms. Meanwhile clean and trim sprouts and cut them in half lengthwise, or quarters if very large.

Melt the butter over medium-high heat in a heavy skillet. Add sprouts, increase heat, and sauté until they begin to brown, stirring occasionally, about 3 to 4 minutes. Sprinkle with sugar, add nuts and salt, and cook, stirring, for another minute. Remove from heat.

Squeeze mushrooms dry, reserving ½ cup of liquid. Cut mushrooms into small pieces, then add to skillet along with the reserved liquid.

Return to low heat, cover, and simmer for 5 minutes or until tender but not mushy. Makes 4 to 6 servings.

Opposite: Pecan trees, planted in favorable conditions and left unpruned, can attain stupendous size. This grizzled old tree is a landmark for horseback riders. Photo courtesy of Hollis Wayne, Happy Horse Hotel, Cedar Creek, Texas.

LANDSCAPE HIGHLIGHTS

- Summer shade
- Fall leaf color
- Winter interest

EDIBLE HIGHLIGHTS

- Nuts shelled and frozen for year-round use
- Baked in entrees and desserts
- Spiced or sugared for snacks

WHERE IT GROWS BEST

- In a large yard, with at least seventy feet square of space
- In warm, humid southern climates with at least 180 frost-free days for nut production
- In deep but light and well-drained soil

HOW TO GROW IT

- As a large, long-lived ornamental tree
- By planting young trees early to nurture long taproot
- With appropriate pest control (see Resources section for Agricultural Extension information about local pest control)
- With other varieties for cross-pollination

Walnut

The walnut tree is one of America's finest hardwood species, and its delicious and richly nutritious nuts form an enjoyable part of the American diet. In the edible landscape, a walnut tree provides open shade, interesting flowers followed by lush foliage, and dazzling autumn color.

Photo © iStockPhoto/Steve Jump.

The black walnut, or *Juglans nigra*, is an American native. So is the closely related butternut, also called white walnut or oilnut, *J. cinerea*.

The walnut tree that produces our familiar supermarket walnut, *J. regia*, is an import, variously called Carpathian walnut, Persian walnut, or, most commonly, English walnut. This tree is grown commercially in California but can also be a wonderful addition to the home garden elsewhere.

My childhood memories of walnuts come from California, where my family lived near the orchards and vineyards planted just outside our hometown. Friends of my parents grew walnuts farther north, and some years we would receive a big burlap sack around Christmas, sewn shut with twine and filled with hundreds of husked walnuts ready to shell. Saturated with flavor, they practically melted in the mouth, but we could never finish all the nuts before the last of them would finally go mealy months later.

Years afterward, traveling in the desolate Central Valley in summer as a young adult, I could mark the location of far-off ranch houses by the presence of tall English walnut trees, which provide the only shade in that flat and blistering landscape. How could those enormous trees live through the cloudless heat, like elephants in a drought? (The answer was well-drained soil and the walnut trees' long taproots seeking the aquifer hidden below.) I came to think of walnut trees as hard, grown by people hard enough to prosper in that difficult land.

Now, living in North Carolina, I relate to the black walnuts instead. They too are hard: hard shelled, with wood prized for its beautiful dusky grain, tight and straight. These walnuts don't grow in manicured groves but rather scattered through the forests of the Appalachians and the moist lowlands beyond.

One of my neighbors here has a huge walnut tree that looms over the western side of my yard—a raucous dwelling place for birds and squirrels. Another neighbor has a walnut tree too. I find the half-shells from both trees scattered all over my yard; the meats have been consumed by animals and only the lovely waste remains.

Marion Cunningham's Walnut Sage Stuffing

1/2 cup butter, melted, divided
1 1/2 cups finely chopped onion
1 1/2 cups finely chopped celery
9 cups bread, dried and broken into small pieces
2 cups coarsely chopped California or other walnuts
3 tablespoons finely chopped fresh sage
1/2 cup finely chopped parsley
1 teaspoon salt
1 teaspoon freshly ground black pepper
1 to 2 cups turkey broth or chicken broth
    (enough to make the mixture moist, not soggy)

Preheat oven to 325 degrees F. Heat 2 tablespoons butter in a skillet over medium heat. Add onions and celery and cook, stirring often, until vegetables are soft but not browned.

Place bread, walnuts, sage, parsley, salt, and pepper in a large bowl. Add onion mixture and the remaining melted butter and toss well. Slowly add the broth, a little at a time, tossing the mixture. Add only enough liquid to moisten.

Transfer the stuffing into a casserole dish with approximately 2 1/2 quart capacity. Cover with foil and bake 45 minutes to an hour.

Tips: To test the stuffing to see if the moisture and seasonings are correct, melt a little butter in a skillet, add a rounded tablespoon of the stuffing and stir until lightly golden. For a livelier flavor, add more sage, onion, salt, and/or pepper.

Yield: 8 cups, or sixteen 1/2-cup servings.

Recipe courtesy of Marion Cunningham for the California Walnut Board.

This hearty stuffing invites improvisation with fresh ingredients from the garden: try nuts, herbs, and perhaps even late-season fruit. Photo courtesy of the California Walnut Board.

LANDSCAPE HIGHLIGHTS

- Summer shade
- Fall leaf color

EDIBLE HIGHLIGHTS

- Nuts shelled for snacking and baking
- Cooked in sauces
- Candied for desserts

WHERE THEY GROW BEST

- In temperate climates with at least 150 frost-free days for nut production, but hardy to sub-zero temperatures
- In full sun
- In a large yard, spaced at least twenty-five feet apart
- In slightly acidic, well-drained soil

HOW TO GROW IT

- As a tall shade tree or pruned for nut production
- With a companion walnut tree for best pollination
- With no competition from weeds or vines
- By pruning only in spring or summer, not when dormant
- Without too much fertilizer

CRACKING THE HULL

A thick, tough husk surrounds the nut's shell, so it's necessary to break the husk off before using the nuts. Some gardeners build a shallow wooden trough just wider than a car's tires, which they lay on a driveway. They lay the husks in the trough and let a car crack the husks apart. Keep the messy husks outdoors.

Photo by Lonnie Webster.

Herbs & Vines

Fruit trees and nut trees, even berries, all live away from the
house. Herbs and vines, in contrast, live close by: snuggled
against the house or garage, sheltering us from summer's heat in
arbors, lining flower beds, trailing along the porch, or filling the
spaces between paving stones, surviving quite nicely in the dead
zone under eaves.

They soften the architectural angles of our lives and give the
garden a comfortable, lived-in look.

We brush up against herbs as we work in the edible landscape—
and stop to savor the aroma. We marvel at their masses of colorful
blossoms and their lush foliage, or at their strong upright, twining
growth and welcoming shade.

Most wondrous of all are the many foods and beverages that are
enhanced by the use of herbs. Herbs and vines give us health not
only as foods, but also as medicines and liniments. Since earliest
civilization, herbs and vines have figured in religious ceremonies;
they are the subjects of prayers and thanksgiving.

Herbs and vines are intimate, warm, and constant. They are close
friends, to us and to each other. Where one thrives, the others tend
to do well, too, and even in surprisingly cold climates it is possible
to nurture some herbs through the winter. With care, we can eat
fresh green herbs in winter and add a little greenery to the landscape as well. In high season, look for carpets of blossoms.

Herbs have such distinctive characteristics. Some love sun, others
shade. Some love poor, gritty, and dry soil, while others like an
almost swampy moisture level. Some love heat and some love cold,
and some don't care. Some like their roots good and hot, while
others want their roots shaded and cool. But they all do best with
organic growing methods.

They can be used in formal or informal settings—grouped together or standing all alone—and in such varied landscape applications as a privacy screen, a decorative accent, or a ground cover.

Vines, especially, require discipline so that they will not become overgrown and lose their productive capacities.

There are too many herbs and vines to describe in a book of this modest size, so I have made selections based on their widest landscape value and usefulness. So, for example, the regal red bee balm, with its tonic health effects and incomparable flower heads, gets left out for two reasons: it can require almost a running stream to keep it alive, and in winter it dies back to the ground and turns to mush.

Likewise the graceful fennel, with its lacy greenery and edible root bulb; this is a summer plant, as is feathery dill, and both are pretty useless in a winter landscape.

I have also left out many tender herbs that are perfect in the kitchen garden but lack pizzazz in the landscape; cilantro is one, basil another.

What remains is a list of herbs and vines that perform well in many parts of the country and that quickly yield quantities of especially useful culinary ingredients.

The sweet bay—or bay tree—is too little used in the landscape and deserves a closer look. Grape vines can last a lifetime and provide juice, wine, edible leaves, and marvelous shade; and grapes can grow almost anywhere. The kiwifruit, in both tender and hardy versions, is relatively new on the North American scene and should get consideration for its lush growth of pink-tinged leaves and its delightful fruit.

Mint, which some consider a scourge, has a role in filling wet, shady expanses, and its uses in the kitchen are limitless. The nasturtium shoots a burst of color into any garden, and the leaves, flowers, and seeds are edible.

The triumvirate of rosemary, sage, and thyme are garden classics. Satisfying to the eye, the nose, and the tongue, they add spice to life.

Robust in any form—low and bushy, tree-like, or pruned into shapes—bay belongs in every cook's garden. Photo by Robin Siktberg of the Herb Society of America.

GROWING PLANTS IN CONTAINERS

Most of the plants in this section of the book, and in the Hot Country Choices section, too, can be grown to bearing size in containers. Container gardening requires using the right equipment and supplies.

One successful hothouse gardener offers some tips for best results: use the largest unglazed containers you can handle (at least five gallons and up to twenty) and utilize a set of wheels if necessary; and, to prevent rot, make sure not to let any water sit in a drainage saucer. Create your own soil mix by starting with high quality potting soil, like Metro Mix, and add pure ingredients to attain correct pH level and soil porosity for each kind of plant (peat, pulverized lime, sand, or even cat litter). Install any plant supports like stakes or trellises to the bottom of the container when filling it with soil. Water the plants frequently and dilute any fertilizer applications. Finally, make sure to leave containers outdoors as many days over 40 degrees F as possible.

Bay Tree

Laurus nobilis, plant of many uses and many names—sweet bay, Greek bay, Roman bay, bay tree, bay laurel.

In ancient Greece and Rome, garlands of the glossy evergreen leaves crowned athletes, generals, and heroes, who then could retire to rest on their laurels. The tree helped ward off evil and danger and promoted health and healing; when a

Modest in appearance, the evergreen bay tree is a valuable addition to the edible landscape. It can grow as a hedge or a specimen tree. Photo by Tim Kozusko.

family's bay tree died, they worried.

The sweet bay belongs in every edible landscape where climate allows, and because the bay grows well as a container plant that can be moved indoors in winter, that's almost anywhere. Its natural climate is Mediterranean, so it will survive some frost, but ideally the bay tree growing outdoors should not be subjected to brutal freeze conditions.

This plant is a handsome relative of the sassafras and avocado, with naturally bushy, almost stiff, foliage. The dark green leaves grow in bunches, with a lighter mid-rib for contrast. Left to itself, the slow-growing bay tree can attain a height of sixty feet, although many sources report that bay only grows as a shrub, fifteen or twenty feet.

The bay responds well to pruning, so it can be planted in multiples and shaped into a hedge, or cut hard into topiary; examples abound of fanciful poufs atop zigzag or spiraling trunks. But for the most part, the bay simply works as a reliable bit of greenery in the herb garden or across the lawn. Inconspicuous cream-colored flowers and dark blue berries are considered a minor part of the bay tree's attraction.

For cooks, the fresh or lightly dried leaves of the bay are indispensable. Their role is to meld and deepen flavors, and they are a standard part of recipes for soups, stews, and even some desserts. The flavor has been described as "pungent and complex—something between eucalyptus, mint, lemon, and fresh-cut grass."

For the price of a few supermarket spice jars of desiccated bay leaves grown far away, the home gardener can buy a sweet bay tree and have fresh, aromatic bay leaves any time at all—and for many, many years to come.

I made that culinary and landscape investment a few years ago, when I was going through a stage of buying nursery stock that could only marginally be called appropriate for the cold mountain climate of western North Carolina. I was trying to "push the envelope," botanically speaking, and my ace in the hole was a sheltered, sunny part of the garden where I felt a bay tree couldn't fail. For the record, the supplier advised that the bay could survive to 0 degrees F, and it did.

Indeed, it grew well near the other herbs in a raised bed in front of the house. When winter came I carefully tucked it in, using a peony cage to hold a stuffing of pine needles. That arrangement kept the elements from the bay tree, and if I needed bay leaves for a recipe, I could push aside the pine needles and snip from the top. When spring came I removed the cage, and the plant perked right up and added new growth.

Bay Syrup

Simple syrup infused with bay leaf can be used for extra flavor on fresh fruit, baked desserts, and cocktails. Recipes are all over the map—literally—with many variations on a common theme that seems to have originated long ago; the one constant is the use of bay leaves, either fresh or dried, or in combination.

To make the syrup, start a day or so ahead. Use two cups granulated sugar to a cup of water, or use some honey as a sugar substitute. Boil until the sugar has dissolved, then pour over 6 to 8 bay leaves in a bowl; some cooks add slivers of lemon peel or bruised juniper berries. Let steep a half hour; then strain through a fine sieve into a jar, cover, and refrigerate.

Pour over pound cake, add to fruit compote or slices of fresh fruit, or use as a flavoring for rum drinks or fruit beverages.

LANDSCAPE HIGHLIGHTS
- Evergreen for year-round interest
- Hedge for screening
- Potted for container gardening

EDIBLE HIGHLIGHTS
- Leaves dried whole for stews and sauces
- Leaves infused for syrup, used in desserts and drinks

WHERE IT GROWS BEST
- Outdoors, in an even climate without much frost, like a coastal zone
- Indoors during winter where a cold climate dictates container gardening
- In sunny but not burning hot or windy locations
- In well-drained soil rich in humus

HOW TO GROW IT
- Outdoors as a small, slow-growing tree
- Massed as a hedge
- Pruned as topiary
- As a prolific evergreen herb

HOW TO MAKE TOPIARY
The ancient art of topiary—sculpting plants into shapes—requires patience and imagination, but it is not difficult. Use clean, sharp tools to shear or carefully clip off small measures of vegetation at a time. Gradually shape the plant over several seasons. Water generously and use diluted fertilizer to ensure the plant's vigor.

Grape

Grape vines have been intertwined with human life for at least six thousand years and have only become more beloved, more varied and widespread, with time. Today in North America there are thousands of choices for grape vines in the edible landscape, all reflecting the local conditions in which they thrive.

Indeed, there is a grape vine for nearly every climate; what they all have in common is the need for sunshine, good air circulation, well-drained and not overly rich soil, and regular pruning. They also share excellent nutritional value, with high antioxidant levels.

Table grapes are pruned every year to encourage fruiting. Still, if left unattended over time they can be reinvigorated without fuss. Photo by Patrick Tregenza, United States Department of Agriculture.

In the edible landscape, grapes provide not only fresh fruit for the table and use in wine and preserves, but also shade in summer and architectural interest in winter. Grape vines are forgiving and can be neglected for years but brought back to life with proper care. They prefer sloping ground that can shed frost, and soil with a lot of grit to aid drainage and retain solar heat.

Most of us are familiar with European grape varieties: table grapes and wine grapes with thin skins that cling tightly to the juicy pulp; many of these are seedless.

There are also native American grapes of two general types: fox grapes, which range mostly in the eastern United States and climb high into the trees, and muscadine grapes, the fat, sweet,

Pickled Grape Leaves

These pickled leaves are best when they have "matured" a few weeks in the jar. Rinse them before using.

Quantities in this hand-me-down recipe are vague, because the number you process will depend on how many young, unblemished grape leaves you harvest. Late in summer the leaves are tough.

2 teaspoons salt in one quart of water for blanching
1 quart water for each jar of leaves
Whole grape leaves, stems snipped off
1 cup bottled lemon juice for each jar of leaves

Wash and sterilize wide-mouth quart canning jars, new lids, bands, and utensils by scalding.

Add salt to quart of water and bring to a boil. Add batches of grape leaves and blanch for 30 seconds, poking them to make sure salted water reaches all surfaces. Drain. Stack grape leaves and form into loose rolls; pack the rolled leaves vertically into jars.

For each jar used, bring a quart of water to boil and add lemon juice. Pour over the packed leaves, leaving 1/2-inch headroom. Gently cover with lids and bands, and seal in a boiling water bath.

Grape Dumplings

1 cup flour
1 1/2 teaspoons baking powder
2 teaspoons sugar
1/4 teaspoon salt

1 tablespoon shortening
1/2 cup grape juice for dough,
    plus sufficient grape juice
    for boiling

Mix flour, baking powder, sugar, and salt. Add shortening. Add juice and mix into stiff dough. Roll dough very thin on floured board and cut into strips 1/2 inch wide (or roll dough in hands and break off pea-sized bits).

Drop into boiling grape juice and cook for 10 to 12 minutes.

Recipe courtesy of the Eastern Band of Cherokee Indians.

thick-skinned grapes of the humid South. However, native grapes have also figured prominently in more westerly localities.

The explorers of the Lewis and Clark expedition of 1804–06 had many auspicious encounters with native grapes. Once, a member of the party got separated for nearly two weeks, lost ahead of the others while low on ammunition. "He had been twelve days without anything to eat but grapes and one rabbit, which he killed by shooting a piece of hard stick in place of a ball," reads one journal entry.

The Crow Indians called wild grapes Slick Bears' Eyes, for the way "you can just see those wild grapes down by the creek shining at you like bears' eyes in the trees," according to writer Alma Hogan Snell. A favorite way of preparing the fruit, besides eating it fresh, was to crush the grapes, seeds, and stems together before making this pulp into patties. These were dried in the sun, and then could be eaten as is or reconstituted and made into sauce.

Grape breeders have mixed characteristics from all kinds of grapes to enlarge the scope of possibility.

LANDSCAPE HIGHLIGHTS

- Over patio or arbor for summer shade
- Winter interest
- Trimmed vines and tendrils useful for crafts

EDIBLE HIGHLIGHTS

- Fruit fresh from the vine
- Canned as juice or jelly
- Dehydrated as raisins
- Leaves pickled for Middle Eastern cuisine

WHERE IT GROWS BEST

- In any climate with summer heat; vines survive from frost-free zones to -40 degrees F, Zone 3, depending on variety
- On a strong arbor or fence, or with a post-and-wire system
- In full sun or slight shade
- In a loose or gritty soil that drains well
- On a slight slope to shed frost

HOW TO GROW IT

- With specific local characteristics (see Resources section for Agricultural Extension information)
- Without too much fertilizer
- Pruned each year for maximum fruit production
- Without overwatering once vines are established
- As a roomy shade house, with brick, stone, or gravel floor
- Along porch railing for support and easy harvest, old-world style

HOW TO PRUNE GRAPE VINES

Without strong pruning during the dormant period, grape vines will put too much of the next year's growth into leaves and vines, and not enough into fruit. Over time the vines become overgrown and unproductive.

Once vines are established they should be pruned every year to keep the proportion of woody vine low in relation to the new growth that can occur; the idea is to remove all but a few buds per branch from the previous season's growth. The stronger an individual plant, the more buds can be left on when pruning. A two-bud cut is standard.

Pruning must be done during winter or vines will "bleed" sap alarmingly. Use clean, sharp tools.

Grapevines left unpruned for many years can be cut back severely to start productive growth again.

Kiwi

The kiwi is sweetness and light, a marvelous addition to any edible landscape and particularly useful in urban settings, where the fast-growing vine can provide attractive screening and, with time, large quantities of fresh fruit.

The kiwi, or kiwifruit, has been called "nutritionally dense"

Kiwi fruits dangle from the vine as they ripen. They are loaded with vitamin C and potassium and rank among the most nutritious fruits. Photo courtesy of USDA/ARS National Clonal Germ Plasm Repository.

and a "nutritional powerhouse" for its vitamin and mineral content. A single kiwi provides a day's requirement of vitamin C; some sources report that one kiwi has twice as much vitamin C as an orange and as much potassium as a banana. Kiwifruit contains magnesium, phosphorous, calcium, iron, zinc, and more.

Not only are kiwis good for you, the inside of the fruit is beautiful and the taste is outstanding. At once smooth and crunchy, the kiwifruit has a creamy, translucent green pulp highlighted with haloes of tiny black seeds and whitish rays. There are gold-colored hybrids on the way.

The flavor has been called a mix of banana, melon, and strawberry. Its slight astringency keeps the kiwifruit from being too sweet, though. Unique, it is a refreshing complement to all sorts of foods and beverages and is equally good as a snack on its own. Mashed, the kiwifruit can be used as a meat tenderizer.

A single mature kiwi vine can produce one hundred pounds of fruit, and the kiwifruit can keep well for months in a cool, dark place.

There are some forty varieties of kiwi in two main types: fuzzy kiwis, which grow in tropical and subtropical climates, and hardy kiwis, some of which can withstand temperatures as low as -40 degrees F.

Perhaps first known as Yang Tao or Yang-tao, the fuzzy kiwi, *Actinidia deliciosa*, originally grew in China's Yangtze River region thousands of years ago, climbing high into the surrounding trees. That's one legend. Another version has the kiwi growing in Japan and India too. At any rate, fuzzy kiwi seeds with the Anglicized

Photo by Nan K. Chase.

Potassium Power Smoothie

1 cup vanilla soy milk, fortified
1 cup orange juice (calcium fortified optional)
2 kiwifruit, washed, unpeeled and chopped
1 banana, sliced
½ cup ice cubes
2 tablespoons soy protein powder
1 teaspoon honey

Blend all ingredients in blender on high for 20 to 30 seconds, or until smooth. Serve immediately.

Makes 2 servings.

Recipe courtesy of ZESPRI Kiwifruit.

Kiwi reveals its inner beauty. The pulp is versatile, offering a combination of sweetness and astringency, smoothness and crunch. Photo ©iStockPhoto/Vladimir Vladimirov.

name "Chinese gooseberries" were sent to New Zealand in the early twentieth century, where they grew in commercial quantities. The Maori word "kiwi" was one of a number of early name changes to gain marketing traction.

In the middle of the twentieth century the plant went to California, where it has also proven a reliable crop. Other places where fuzzy kiwifruit is grown commercially will tell you what kind of climate it likes: Italy, Chile, France, Greece, Iran.

For the rest of us, in cooler regions, there's the hardy kiwifruit. Hardy kiwis can take lower temperatures and they have less sensitivity to early and late frosts.

Where the fuzzy kiwi grows to about thirty feet in height—if permitted—the hardy kiwi tops out lower, about twenty feet. The leaves of the hardy kiwi are smaller and less leathery than those of the fuzzy kiwi, only some two to five inches long instead of eight or ten; the male of the super-hardy Arctic Beauty kiwi, *A. kolomikta*, has beautiful leaves, with tips and edges that turn pink as the vine matures.

The biggest difference between the fuzzy and hardy kiwis is the fruit. Fuzzy kiwi has fuzzy fruit, while the hardy kiwi is hairless, smaller, and sweeter. In either case the skin is edible.

LANDSCAPE HIGHLIGHTS

- Screening during frost-free months
- Interesting leaf colors

EDIBLE HIGHLIGHTS

- Fresh fruit from the vine, keeps well
- Sliced in fruit salads and smoothies

WHERE IT GROWS BEST

- On a trellis, fence, or arbor for support
- In warm or moderate climates for fuzzy kiwi (survives to about 0 degrees F) or cold climates for hardy kiwi (to -40 degrees F, Zone 3, depending on variety)
- In sun or partial shade, depending on variety
- In fertile, well-drained soil

HOW TO GROW IT

- As a vigorous fruiting vine that grows at least fifteen feet tall and equally wide
- With a male plant and at least one female plant; consult a nursery for proper ordering
- For a bearing age of three to four years after planting

TRELLISES AND ARBORS

The kiwi's prolific leaf growth and heavy fruit production—all in vine form—make it a dense, heavy plant. A vertical structure will help keep vegetation off the ground, where it is susceptible to rot. A trellis (built upright against a fence or building) or an arbor (big enough to sit or walk beneath) should not call attention to itself but be well anchored and have strong joints and plenty of open spaces for healthy stem and leaf growth. Wooden structures should be left unpainted to reduce chemical contamination.

Lavender

Crush lavender blossoms in your hand, inhale deeply, and you'll understand the age-old allure of this beautiful aromatic herb.

Lavender, dried or fresh, has a long history of calming nerves, banishing insects, freshening linens, cleansing wounds,

This page and opposite: Lavender, like other herbs in the edible landscape, draws bees into the garden and enhances pollination for many other plants. Photos courtesy of Mountain Farm, Burnsville, North Carolina.

stopping toothaches, and performing a host of other valuable functions. The root of its Roman name, *Lavandula,* means "to wash," and in addition to a body wash, lavender has proved an essential ingredient in many perfumes and colognes.

Even more than a culinary herb—although in moderation it adds piquancy to all sorts of food and drink—lavender has a place in the home medicine chest. When grown organically and then carefully cleaned and dried, lavender blossoms keep well and can retain their incomparable fragrance and their potency for years.

Bushy silver-grey foliage lightens the edible landscape in tone, and the profuse spikes of lavender flowers, which can range from white to deepest purple, cause a sensation when they bloom. Its moderate height, from about one to four feet tall, makes lavender a good companion in formal plantings.

Bees and butterflies love lavender, which enhances pollination in the edible landscape. One observer wrote that lavender makes the air "vibrate with wings." Although the blossoms are commonly cut and used in summer months, seed heads left through the winter provide a favorite food for birds.

In warm regions lavender grows almost as an evergreen, and parts of the West Coast offer the perfect combination of intense sunshine and light, in addition to warm soil. There lavender flourishes in colorful swaths around countryside and city alike, and the Pacific states are home to many fine lavender farms. No wonder, for lavender has its roots in the Mediterranean region, where the soil and climate are much the same.

Surprisingly, then, lavender can also grow well and bloom in much cooler climates. The secret is to replicate a microclimate of similar characteristics.

Marilyn Cade has made a miracle happen in the cold, damp (but darkly beautiful) Appalachian Mountains of western North Carolina, where she raises lavender and dairy goats on twenty-four very steep acres.

Here are her rules for getting lavender to grow and produce anywhere: the plants require at least six hours of direct sun daily and dry heat, and also need good air circulation and soil drainage; in fact, the soil should have no added organic mulches or even much nutrition.

Mountain Farm Citrus Lavender Marinade

¾ cup white wine (or lavender) vinegar

¼ cup lemon zest (1 to 1½ large lemons)

¼ cup fresh lemon juice

1¾ teaspoons fresh lime juice

¼ cup orange juice

¼ cup extra virgin olive oil

⅓ cup lavender honey

1 tablespoon culinary lavender (dried organic lavender blossoms)

2 teaspoons salt

⅛ tablespoon black pepper

Combine all ingredients and mix well before adding meat or tofu.
Refrigerate meat or tofu in marinade for at least four hours for best flavor.

Recipe courtesy of Mountain Farm, Burnsville, North Carolina.

Lavender thrives with full sun and good drainage, even in colder parts of North America. The plant dislikes rich soil, preferring gravel or stones. Photo by Robin Siktberg of the Herb Society of America.

She adds that lavender should be planted near rocks, gravel, or dry stone pathways and should be watered sparingly to avoid mildew. If the soil is on the acid side, sweeten it with lime. The flowers should be harvested early, as the first few buds have opened, and the stems cut as long as possible (this is the time to "strip" flowers for use in potpourri and sachets or to prepare for culinary use). Prune lavender lightly in late winter.

Other gardeners over the centuries have put it more succinctly: lavender thrives on neglect.

It may take several years for lavender plants to mature, especially in a cooler climate, but the bushes get large individually rather than running.

As a culinary herb, lavender blossoms are used to flavor salt, sugar, vinegar, and syrups for family-friendly or adult beverages, to name just a few. The traditional "herbes de Provence" consist of lavender mixed with marjoram, thyme, rosemary, basil, bay leaf, and sometimes fennel seed, with thyme predominating.

LANDSCAPE HIGHLIGHTS

- Spring and summer blooms
- Attracts bees and butterflies
- Light-colored foliage for garden contrast
- Winter food for birds

EDIBLE HIGHLIGHTS

- Infused for flavored vinegar, salt, sugar, syrup
- Woody stalks used as kebab skewers
- Flavoring for stews
- Flowers decorate salads

WHERE IT GROWS BEST

- In a warm or moderate climate
- In thin, gritty soil that drains well
- In full sun
- Along pathways, in rock gardens, on terraces

HOW TO GROW IT

- As a low-growing decorative herb, mounding rather than running by roots
- With little watering or feeding, but occasional removal of dead woody stems
- As a soft grey-blue evergreen in warmer locations
- With lime added to the soil to sweeten it

Mint

D on't plant mint! It takes over the garden.
That's an all-too-common reaction, and it's true that some mint varieties can run wild if given the right soil, moisture, and sunlight, but no discipline.

I say hurray for mint.

Mint grows in a mind-boggling array of shapes, colors, even flavors. This Hillary's Sweet Lemon Mint prefers a cool, shady location. Photo by Robin Siktberg of the Herb Society of America.

A pretty, low-growing plant, mint fills in the wet, shady places where nothing else will grow. And while the flowers are generally not flashy, they do add lacy pastel highlights to the summer garden and attract beneficial insects.

Mint's medicinal properties have been chronicled for centuries, and its usefulness in the kitchen is reflected in the fact that cookbooks of ancient Rome contained mint recipes. In houses and temples of those times, mint leaves were strewn over the floors to freshen the air as people walked.

The Spanish name for mint, *yerba buena,* means the "good herb." Mint effectively calms the stomach and aids digestion (after-dinner mint, anyone?). It calms nerves, too, and is used in compresses for the relief of skin and joint problems, as well as for headaches and sore eyes.

In my own edible landscape it has taken ten years for a nice little mint patch to get started, and now that it shows signs of robustness (discipline time), I have started using it for cooking and tea, and most spectacularly, for making mint wine.

Peppermint and spearmint. Apple mint and chocolate mint. Curly mint and creeping mint and long-stemmed mint. There are a dozen main mint species and hundreds of hybrids. Sizes range from only a few inches high to some two feet or more.

All these members of the genus *Mentha* have square stems as a distinguishing characteristic.

They also have a tendency to "run," so unless you have room for the mint to naturalize, plan early to contain the plants in sunken boxes or pots, or by using lengths of metal or plastic edging to a depth of six or eight inches.

Wild Mint Tea

1 quart water
1 cup mint leaves and blossoms
Honey or sugar (optional)

Boil the water and add the mint leaves and blossoms. Let set for 20 minutes. Add honey or sugar to taste, if desired. Serve.

Reprinted from A Taste of Heritage: Crow Indian Recipes and Herbal Medicines *by Alma Hogan Snell by permission of the University of Nebraska Press. ©2006 by Alma Hogan Snell.*

Mint Wine

1 packet regular yeast

7 pounds sugar, depending on sweetness desired

3 gallons water

3 quarts tightly packed mint leaves, cleaned of stems and dirt
(start with twice that amount)

Begin with a clean 5-gallon glass carboy for fermentation and scald any utensils you need. Fill the carboy with a solution of 1 tablespoon household bleach per gallon of cold water. Let this stand 20 minutes, empty, and then rinse the carboy three times with cold water.

In a quart jar, combine 1½ cups lukewarm water (114 degrees F) with the yeast, and set in a warm place as you prepare the other ingredients. It should be frothy.

Make a syrup of the sugar with 3 gallons of water, and boil five minutes, or until the sugar is completely dissolved. Meanwhile, bruise the mint leaves and stuff them into the carboy; then pour the syrup over the leaves and let the mixture stand until it cools to lukewarm.

Add the yeast mixture to the carboy and swirl it to distribute. Seal the top loosely with a piece of plastic wrap and a rubber band, or with a brewer's S-shaped "water trap." Store the carboy in a dark place about 65 degrees F and let it ferment undisturbed until all bubbling stops, about 2 to 3 months. When the mint leaves fall away and the wine is clear, gently siphon the fermented wine into clean bottles that have been sterilized 20 minutes in a 1 tablespoon to 1 gallon bleach and water solution. Consult a home brew supplier about capping options.

Let wine sit another few weeks for further clarification.

Recipe adapted from Folk Wines, Cordials, & Brandies *by M. A. Jagendorf (1963, The Vanguard Press, Inc.).*

Crystal clear and with just a hint of mint flavor, homemade mint wine makes a delightful summer beverage and an unusual gift. Photo by Nan K. Chase.

LANDSCAPE HIGHLIGHTS
- Blankets moist, shady ground
- Lacy flowers attract insects

EDIBLE HIGHLIGHTS
- Infused for tea, syrup, vinegar
- Dried for winter use
- Produces delicate wine
- Delightful in salads, chutney, and cooked vegetables or meat

WHERE IT GROWS BEST
- In moist soil
- In full or partial shade, full sun only with sufficient moisture

HOW TO GROW IT
- With roots contained in a below-ground box or pot, or behind concrete or metal barriers underground to prevent unwanted spreading
- In poor soil to discourage spread; rich soil promotes "running"
- Away from tree trunks and other plants. Mint doesn't mix well with other plants, as mint leaves form a mat.

Nasturtium

We love the nasturtium for its versatility in the edible landscape. Nasturtium is nearly foolproof to grow, yet as a culinary herb it remains underutilized.

All visible parts of the plant are edible—flowers, leaves, even seeds—and its foliage and flowers flow through the garden like a river of color.

The nasturtium's color spectrum ranges from off-white through shades of yellow and orange to pink and red—great contrast to a weather-beaten fence or building. Photo by Lonnie Webster.

In looks, the nasturtium is part vine, part ground cover. There are some fifty varieties, so shop for characteristics you like.

Generally the leaves are a few inches across, round and light green with white rays, and with a smooth, velvety feel: like small water-lily pads. The leaves of the climbing varieties (as opposed to dwarf varieties) have a twining habit that helps them grab onto support structures.

The flowers are bold and bright, with a long, graceful, funnel-shaped spur at the bottom: orange, yellow, or red, in countless combinations.

Nasturtiums play several useful roles, providing fast screening of unsightly features, organic pest protection, garden infill after spring bulbs fade, and cascading texture and color in window boxes and other containers.

Easily grown from seed, the nasturtium—or *Tropaeolum*—thrives in most climates. In warm zones it survives year-round, but in cold-weather regions it must be sown each spring. Germination of the easy-to-handle seeds takes just seven to ten days, making it a perfect child's garden project.

The nasturtium is not fussy about soil, but it prefers a well-drained location with a sandy component rather than too much leaf mold. While it can grow in both shade and sun, you'll get masses of flowers in a sunny location, but mostly foliage in shady or wet ground.

Aphids are drawn to nasturtiums, nestling under the leaves. That makes them an important companion plant for roses, as nasturtiums draw the aphids away. They can also repel some kinds of flies and beetles. "Nasturtium spray" for bug control is made like tea from equal parts nasturtium leaves and water, boiled fifteen minutes,

Photo by Nan K. Chase.

Pickled Nasturtium Seeds

Recipes for pickled nasturtium seeds vary widely, so here's a version that combines elements from several sources. It's difficult to specify quantities of ingredients, as the amount of seeds will differ.

Pick the seedpods on a dry day before they ripen—still green and plump—leaving a bit of stem attached. Soak pods for three days in saltwater (2 to 4 tablespoons salt to a quart), changing the water daily; then rinse and dry. Pack pods loosely into a small jar and measure enough white wine vinegar, cider vinegar, or lavender vinegar to cover, but put the vinegar into a small saucepan instead of the jar.

Make spiced vinegar by adding small quantities of spices and seasonings to the pan: bay leaves, thyme, tarragon, grated horseradish, shallots, ground mace, grated nutmeg, or similar. For each jar, add 2 teaspoons sugar and half a dozen black or white peppercorns.

Bring the vinegar and spice mixture to a boil; then pour over nasturtium pods in the jar. Let cool. Cover and refrigerate for at least three days before using.

Pickled seedpods will keep in the refrigerator six months.

As they grow thicker, nasturtium leaves weave a carpet that can transform an unattractive corner of the garden. Photo by Robin Siktberg of the Herb Society of America.

cooled, and strained.

The flavor of nasturtium leaves is peppery; it is known also as Indian cress. A little bit goes a long way, so the leaves are chopped or torn and sprinkled into salads; the flowers go into salads, too. Nasturtium leaves reportedly contain ten times the vitamin C of lettuce.

The leaves can also be used as wrappers for making little appetizer rolls of herbed cream cheese or other spreads. Minced nasturtium leaves add pep to egg dishes.

Creative cooks find no end of uses for this plant: nasturtium mayonnaise, nasturtium vinegar, and pepper made from the dried and ground seeds. The blossoms can be stuffed with soft spreads and served as dainty hors d'oeuvres, or they make an elegant garnish on cakes.

The most sophisticated culinary use of nasturtiums may be as "faux capers" or "poor man's capers." For this simple concoction the unripe seed pods are pickled in spiced vinegar. They, too, contain appreciable levels of vitamin C.

LANDSCAPE HIGHLIGHTS

- Lush ground cover, attractive vine
- Profuse bright flowers in frost-free months
- Nasturtium "tea" as insect repellent

EDIBLE HIGHLIGHTS

- Leaves and flowers for salads
- Leaves added to eggs, mayonnaise, vinegar
- Seed pods pickled as "poor man's capers"

WHERE IT GROWS BEST

- In full sun for maximum flower production, in shade for mostly leaf growth
- In well-drained soil for flowers, in damp ground for foliage
- In fertile soil with compost added to break up clumps

HOW TO GROW IT

- As climbing vines to twelve feet or lush groundcover, depending on variety
- As an annual from seed in cool or cold climates, as a perennial in frost-free zones
- As a companion to roses and potted citrus, since nasturtium attracts aphids to itself and provides organic pest control

Rosemary, Sage, Thyme

Ah, the strange perfume of rosemary: dense, penetrating, and unforgettable. And so *Rosmarinus officinalis*, called "dew of the sea" for its native habitat along Mediterranean cliffs, is the herb of memory.

Sage, too, has a peculiar aroma, and silvery blue-grey leaves

Unobtrusive rosemary softens hard edges around the landscape. The attractive blue-grey foliage can reach as high as six feet. Photo by Jamie Goodman.

in contrast to rosemary's dark, glossy, needle-like foliage.

Thyme, small and with a less "pushy" odor than the others, rounds out a trio of important herbs in the edible landscape. Oregano and marjoram could be included, for all are members of the mint family, distinguished by their square stems and their culinary and medicinal roles in human society.

All these herbs add a pleasing, billowy texture to a garden's lower levels, and in many parts of the United States they can grow year round as long as they have enough drainage to keep their feet dry in cold weather. I have harvested thyme and sage in winter, digging through snow to snip off the still-green leaves for cooking.

Rosemary is the tallest, growing from about one foot high to six feet in some cases, but it is also the most tender. Whereas sage and thyme can both survive temperatures as low as -20 degrees F, rosemary can't usually handle anything below 15 degrees F.

Thus, depending on where you live, rosemary might be grown as a perennial hedge or permanent rock garden specimen—California's ideal climate nurtures countless beautiful examples—or as a seasonal plant to be potted up and brought indoors for the winter.

Rosemary has light violet-blue flowers that attract bees and other insects; honey from rosemary-fueled bees has a pleasant flavor. A tea made from the leaf tips can relieve headache. In cooking, rosemary accompanies lamb and other meats and seasons stews and sauces.

Rosemary likes an alkaline soil. As with the other woody herbs mentioned here, it should be pruned sparingly—just enough to remove the oldest branches when they lose vigor, and in no cases more than a third of the plant at once.

Sage grows to a middle height between rosemary and thyme, and brings a feeling of lightness into corners of the garden where darker plants threaten to overwhelm the scenery. The culinary sage of the edible landscape, *Salvia officinalis*, has leaves described as "white, woolly, and wrinkled," and pretty purple flowers, but there are lots

Sage can be a show-off in the edible landscape, massing in low-growing clumps. This variegated sage, with hints of purple, makes a striking accent. Photo by Robin Siktberg of the Herb Society of America.

Nan's Fresh Herb Popovers

The secret of great popovers is to put the greased muffin tin in the oven while it preheats. A perfect crust forms when batter hits the hot oil.

1 cup milk

4 eggs (or 5 if muffin tin is large)

1/4 teaspoon salt

2 tablespoons vegetable oil, plus oil for muffin tin

1 cup flour

1/4 cup or more of finely chopped spring herbs: any combination of thyme, rosemary, sage, oregano, fennel greens, tarragon, parsley, chives, or others

2 to 4 tablespoons chopped onions (optional)

Preheat oven to 400 degrees F with greased muffin tin inside. Combine milk, eggs, salt, and oil. Add flour and whisk until smooth. Add herbs and onions if desired, and whisk to combine.

Fill muffin tin cups 1/2 to 2/3 full, and then bake in the center of the oven 30 to 40 minutes, or until popovers are golden brown and fragrant. Do not open the oven door while baking. Serve immediately.

Low to the ground, thyme still adds a lot of color and texture when in full bloom. The leaves can be used almost as liberally as salt. Photo by Robin Siktberg of the Herb Society of America.

of other varieties.

Superb in stews and stuffing or roasted with meats, sage leaves are best harvested before the flower spikes appear. The name *Salvia* comes from the root word "I save," and the late folklore historian and wine expert M. A. Jagendorf wrote that sage "prolonged life, brightened the spirits, eased sorrow, kept toads away, averted chills, and enabled girls to see their future husbands."

Thyme grows low in the garden and works well as a groundcover on patios and outdoor stairways, where it can run between paving stones. The leaves are tiny, and the plant usually grows less than a foot tall. "Happiness, health, and bravery" are the qualities long ascribed to thyme; in ancient Greece the leaves were spread over the floors of temples and homes, and it was burned as incense.

Thyme seasons soups and sauces—no use making pizza without it—and adds a gentle savor to just about anything else too.

LANDSCAPE HIGHLIGHTS

- Spring and summer blossoms
- Year-round ground covers in low-frost environments
- Thrive in thin soil
- Foliage adds texture in flower beds

EDIBLE HIGHLIGHTS

- Fresh or dried in stews, soups, sauces, dressings, and breads
- Infused for vinegars

WHERE THEY GROW BEST

- Outdoors in frost-free zones for rosemary, light to moderate frost environments for others
- In containers for year-round enjoyment in cold climates, outdoors with sufficient snow cover for insulation
- In well-drained thin or gritty soil
- In full sun
- In rock gardens, on terraces, in raised beds with good drainage

HOW TO GROW THEM

- As companions to taller, more colorful plants
- Near the kitchen, for convenient culinary use

Hot-Country Choices

Fruiting plants that grow in hot climates have exotic flowers, wonderful smells, and unusual fruits. It's as though the orchard trees of North America's temperate zones are all business, while the hot country plants have time to play.

The five plants described in this section (counting the citrus fruits as one) can survive close to desert conditions, but they do require considerable water in order to thrive and produce fruit. The kumquat, by contrast, prefers a fairly moist tropical climate but can grow well in any hot weather if watered sufficiently.

That doesn't mean these plants will only grow in the hottest places, for in many cooler parts of North America they do well in pots that can be brought indoors for protection; plants like the fig and even the pomegranate can grow in cooler climates if they are planted against a sunny wall or insulated for winter, although they might not bloom or bear reliably.

Certainly in well-managed hothouses or conservatories that can nearly replicate these plants' preferred growing conditions, they will attain considerable size and become fruitful.

I think it worthwhile trying to grow these plants in fairly cool regions even if it costs some effort in providing microclimates they can tolerate or in keeping them healthy in containers.

Why? These fruits are important, both nutritionally and for their marvelous flavors and textures. Some of them only ripen on the tree or vine, and thus are almost never shipped long distances to grocery stores; the only way to enjoy them fresh—at their peak of flavor and potency—is to grow them yourself. Many American families of Mediterranean or Middle Eastern heritage have discovered this already, as when they insist on curing their own home-grown olives, for example.

Photo © iStockPhoto/DylanDesigns.

Thus, using these plants in the edible landscape can add a sense of adventure or whimsy, and can give you a reputation as a gourmet cook who always has some tasty and hard-to-get treasure on hand. A dish made with fresh organic Meyer lemons is unforgettable, as is one with fresh figs or a kumquat from the backyard.

Growing any of these hot country choices for the edible landscape is a form of time travel.

The fig and the olive both figure prominently in ancient history, and their culture is a way of life across the Mediterranean region; today both plants are grown commercially in parts of the United States as well.

The juicy pomegranate has a Spanish city named for it—Granada—on a high, dry plateau, and the local symbol there is the image of a ripening pomegranate fruit.

Lemons, limes, oranges, and other citrus fruits have spilled from their Old World territory to become dietary and economic mainstays of several American states. Kumquat will be a new selection for some gardeners.

We love these foods, these handsome and distinctive plants. Now let's try growing them.

Fig

Fig leaves clothed Adam and Eve in the Garden.
The Greek philosopher Plato was a "friend of the fig," a *philosykos*. Captain Bligh sailed the South Seas with fig trees to plant, and the Spanish fathers cultivated them at their California missions.

Figs are one of mankind's favorite fruits, and yet few of us actually know the joys of eating one fresh. The reason: figs are unusual in ripening only on the tree, and when they're

Rangy and exotic, fig trees—or bushes, as they are sometimes grown—have their flowers inside the fruiting structure. Photo by David Karp, United States Department of Agriculture.

fully ripe they are too easily damaged to ship. Perfect for the edible landscape.

Well, perfect if you can provide the necessary warmth. Figs require a long period of warm weather for fruiting, and they can't handle the kind of hard freeze that many other fruits withstand.

The coldest climate where figs can grow and bear outdoors is considered to be that of central Virginia. Even there, fig trees are planted against sheltered, sunny walls and may be lowered to the ground and covered, or heavily wrapped, for winter

Roasted Duck with Dried-Fruit Chutney

2 ducks (about 5 pounds each)
Kosher salt
4 cups dried fruit such as figs (quartered), currants, cherries, and raisins
⅓ cup brown sugar
1 tablespoon molasses
¼ teaspoon red pepper flakes
½ teaspoon black pepper
½ cup orange juice
1 cup water
½ cup cider vinegar

To prepare the duck: remove the necks, hearts, livers, and gizzards; reserve for other uses. Place both ducks in an 11-quart pot, cover with cold water, season with 1 tablespoon salt and bring water to a boil. Remove the pot from the heat and let cool until ducks are cool enough to handle. Remove ducks from the pot and pat dry. Place on a wire rack set over a baking sheet, sprinkle generously with salt, cover, and refrigerate overnight or up to 3 days.

Preheat the oven to 375 degrees F. Place ducks on a rack in a roasting pan large enough to hold both. Add water to come about ½ inch up the sides of the pan (but not so high that it touches the ducks). Place in the oven and roast until the internal temperature of the legs registers 150 degrees F on an instant-read thermometer, 1 hour 15 minutes to 1½ hours. Add water to the pan as needed as it evaporates (pan should not be dry).

Increase oven heat to 475 degrees F and continue roasting the ducks until the skin crisps, about 5 minutes more. Then turn and roast 5 to 10 minutes more to crisp the skin all over. Remove ducks from the oven and let rest 20 minutes.

While the duck is roasting, make the chutney: combine all the remaining ingredients except the vinegar in a saucepan and simmer over low heat until dry, 15 to 20 minutes. Stir in the vinegar and let cool to room temperature.

To carve the duck, cut the legs off the body; cut each leg in half. Cut the breast meat off the ducks and slice. Serve each guest some sliced breast meat and a piece of leg, with the dried-fruit chutney and bread.

Recipe courtesy of Bill Telepan, owner and chef, Telepan Restaurant, New York City.

insulation; colder than that, and figs must grow in containers and be over-wintered indoors.

Figs' main growing requirements are excellent drainage and soil that's "not too rich." When given excess nitrogen, fig trees—or bushes—produce rampant vegetation and not much fruit. Favored soil conditions tend toward the gritty or chalky—anything loose and able to shed moisture quickly.

Likewise, unrestricted root growth can make fig trees a pest. The tree grows at least as wide as tall, and roots may extend far beyond that. Edible landscape gardeners, then, must practice root pruning or create a root barrier underground about five feet from the trunk, if a fig tree is to be grown near a structure.

Planted in a wide open space, a fig tree can grow about thirty feet high and provide wonderful shade. Just as commonly, though, figs for fruit production are grown near a wall, where they can be trained to maximum effect.

Pruning figs is tricky. Too much cutting and they go wild with new branches. Too little and they stagnate. The happy medium is to cut away only weak wood and superfluous shoots; one source advises pruning away about 30 percent of branches every year, leaving a strong, open structure.

There are no visible flowers on fig trees; rather, the flowers of this "inside out" fruit are contained within the receptacle that eventually becomes the fruit. The developing interior seeds give figs their crunch. Pollinators—often a specific wasp—must crawl inside the fig to do their work.

Photo ©·iStockPhoto/UncleScrooge.

LANDSCAPE HIGHLIGHTS

- Dramatic specimen tree in warmer zones
- Potted for container gardening

EDIBLE HIGHLIGHTS

- Fresh fruit from the tree
- Baked in main dishes and desserts
- Dried for long-term use
- Canned as preserves

WHERE IT GROWS BEST

- Most productive in a warm, Mediterranean-type climate, but can survive to 0 degrees F, depending on variety; Desert King and Brown Turkey have good results in cooler climates
- In any well-drained soil
- In full sun

HOW TO GROW IT

- As the ornamental focal point of a large yard

- Lightly pruned, as a small fruiting tree
- In a large container during winter or for small-space gardening (see "Growing Plants in Containers," page 69)
- With winter insulation if left outdoors in cold zones
- With roots contained by root pruning or barrier system

Kumquat

I wish I still had a kumquat tree in the backyard, as I did when I was a young child. We lived in hot country then—Fresno, California—where miles of irrigation ditches criss-crossed the flat, scorching countryside to carry life-giving water to the orchards.

Kumquats are citrus plants, but they are not closely related to oranges or lemons. They have an unusually piquant flavor. Photo by Michelle Levy Brocco, www.mishmishcards.com.

Even as a three- or four-year-old I remember my family's kumquat tree—more like a bush, really—as a patch of cool, dark green leaves in the shade of our plum trees. I remember the bite-size orange fruits, which my sister and I and our friends, barefoot and blissful, would eat right from the branches.

The kumquat's charm was that we ate the thin, sweet skin and spit out the sour fruit and seeds. What a crazy fruit!

Today, if I had a kumquat tree, I would still appreciate its compact form, its glossy evergreen leaves, and its marvelous fruit. But I would pay more attention to the masses of fragrant,

Cranberry Kumquat Sauce

Makes about 2½ cups

2 cups kumquats (9 to 10 ounces), trimmed
¾ cup sugar
¾ cup water
1 (12-ounce) bag fresh or frozen cranberries (3½ cups)

Prick kumquats 2 or 3 times with a sharp fork. Cover kumquats generously with cold water in a heavy medium saucepan and bring to a boil. Drain and rinse with cold water, then repeat 2 more times (to remove bitterness).

Bring kumquats, sugar, and water (¾ cup) to a boil in rinsed saucepan (liquid will not cover kumquats) over high heat, stirring until sugar has dissolved; then reduce heat and gently simmer, uncovered, stirring occasionally, 15 minutes. Remove from heat and cool kumquats in syrup, about 20 minutes.

Transfer kumquats with a slotted spoon to a bowl, reserving syrup in saucepan. Add cranberries and ¼ teaspoon salt to syrup and bring to a boil over high heat, stirring occasionally; then reduce heat and simmer, uncovered, stirring occasionally, until berries burst, 8 to 12 minutes. Remove from heat.

While cranberries cook, quarter kumquats lengthwise, discarding any seeds.

Stir kumquats into cranberry mixture and transfer to a bowl. Cool completely, stirring occasionally, about 30 minutes.

star-shaped white flowers and to the kumquat's great culinary value in the edible landscape.

Kumquats can be used in an astonishing range of foods and beverages. As a citrus fruit, although of a different genus than oranges and lemons, kumquats impart a tangy, sweet-sour flavor to roasted meat, poultry, or seafood; to sauces, glazes, and chutneys; and to cakes and cookies.

Kumquats make spectacular marmalade, and they can flavor vodka, brandy, or other liquors. They can be packed in salt and left to pickle themselves; this unusual treat can last for years in the jar. And they can be candied or preserved in syrup.

When you eat kumquats fresh from the tree, be sure to roll the fruit to release the most flavor from the skin into the fruit. When you pick them to bring indoors, leave a bit of stem attached to lengthen shelf life.

The greatest nutritional content includes vitamin C, of course, but also vitamin A, calcium, potassium, phosphorus, magnesium, and trace elements.

On its own, the kumquat, of the genus *Fortunella,* prefers the climate of Southeast Asia, California, Florida, or Texas, but it can thrive anywhere in a large tub or pot, producing abundant crops of the bite-size fruit through the winter. Topping out at ten to fifteen feet, like a mini-orange tree, it makes a perfect candidate for container gardening in northern zones.

Actually there are four kinds of kumquat, two or three of them readily available as nursery stock in the United States.

The Nagami kumquat is cold-hardy, withstanding occasional temperatures as low as 10 degrees F. This is the common, elongated variety, with the famous sweet skin and sour insides; closely related is the Maruni kumquat. The Meiwa, also cold-hardy, has round fruit with a sweet flavored pulp and less-appealing skin.

Imaginative hybridizing has produced such oddities as the limequat, orangequat, and mandarinquat. Bon appétit!

LANDSCAPE HIGHLIGHTS

- Evergreen in warmer zones
- Potted for container gardening
- Fragrant white flowers, colorful orange fruit

EDIBLE HIGHLIGHTS

- Fresh fruit from the tree
- Flavoring for liquors
- Cooked as marmalade
- Candied for dessert

WHERE IT GROWS BEST

- Outdoors (in frost-free or low-frost zones only); plant in spring
- In a container in colder climates
- Massed in low hedges
- In healthy loam
- In sun or light shade

HOW TO GROW IT

- As a shrub or small tree to fifteen feet
- With plenty of water
- Pruned heavily after winter fruit harvest
- Hand-pollinated with small paintbrush if plants are indoors a lot

Lemon, Lime, Orange

There are so many kinds of citrus fruit—thanks to natural variety and hybrids—that it no longer makes sense to limit the topic to the standard lemons, limes, and oranges.

Today the list of wonderful citrus fruits includes tangerines, tangelos, mandarins, clementines, and others.

Photo by Nan K. Chase.

Grapefruit, of course, is another important citrus fruit but in the edible landscape its larger size may be a deterrent, since it doesn't lend itself as easily to container gardening for colder climates.

What they all have in common are glossy, dark-green leaves, beautiful and fragrant flowers, delicious and intensely nutritious fruits, a need for well-drained soil and ample sunlight, and intolerance of cold temperatures.

Virtually all of them are evergreen. The cold-weather sour orange—*Poncirus trifoliata* or Flying Dragon—is an exception, and often provides zone-expanding root stock for other citrus.

Grow citrus trees in the ground only where temperatures stay above freezing (or only get a few degrees of frost). In colder regions, consider growing them in pots; even in hot country, some gardeners grow citrus in pots to decorate patios.

A splash of fresh Meyer lemon juice improves any dish. With year-round appeal, this lovely plant does well in porous containers. ©iStockPhoto/ Terry Wilson.

Every edible landscape gardener should grow citrus, just to forego the industrial waxes and fungicides that coat most supermarket citrus. I have never forgotten the penetrating chemical smell hanging over a citrus packing plant during a school field trip in Orange County, California; now, when I get a bag of fresh lemons from my niece's organic backyard tree near San Francisco, they look, feel, smell, and taste better than anything store-bought. They're juicier, too.

My gardening buddy Doc has perfected a method for growing small citrus trees in pots. He divides his gardening time between the Blue Ridge Mountains and the Hudson River Valley—hardly citrus country—but his potted trees are usually lush with fruit. Meyer lemon is the most prolific.

"Use a good commercial potting mix without fertilizers or water crystals," he advises. "Then you need a big unglazed terra-cotta pot and water, water, water."

Since citrus can bloom and bear fruit year round, he advises fairly constant feeding with a blooming formula. Keep pots outdoors as long as possible each year, so plants get pollinated, and be ready to hand-pollinate with a small paintbrush during winter months indoors. "And don't be impatient. It can take a full year from bloom to fruit."

He also cautions gardeners to keep potted citrus from sunburn by placing pots on the eastern side of a building or in an open northern setting; commercial growers sometimes whitewash tree trunks for this purpose, and paper wrapping is available also.

My only current citrus is the incredibly twisted and thorny trifoliate orange, the Flying Dragon. It provides awesome year-round screening and, yes, even fruit: the sour orange. One humorous recipe for "Poncirus-ade" calls for "a barrel of water, a barrel of sugar, and one sour fruit."

Orange-Almond Pancakes

Pancakes

1 cup sliced almonds	¾ cup buckwheat flour
1 whole orange	1 cup all-purpose flour
1 egg	1 tablespoon baking powder
⅔ cup orange juice	¼ teaspoon salt
1 cup 2-percent reduced fat milk	Non-stick cooking spray
2 tablespoons grapeseed or canola oil	

Preheat oven to 375 degrees F. Spread almonds over a baking sheet and bake 5 to 7 minutes until nicely browned. Remove and cool at room temperature. Use grater to grate zest of orange while careful not to grate into the white pith. Peel remainder of skin and slice between membranes to separate each orange segment. Set aside for garnish.

Combine egg, orange juice, milk, and oil in a medium bowl and mix well. In a large bowl, combine both flours, baking powder, and salt with reserved orange zest. Add liquid into the dry ingredients and mix thoroughly while being sure to leave some lumps.

Set aside ¼ cup almonds for syrup, then gently mix remaining ¾ cup almonds into batter until ingredients are combined, but still lumpy. Do not over-beat or stir until smooth, as this will make pancakes tough.

Ladle batter onto a hot non-stick skillet coated with cooking spray and cook until some bubbles begin to appear on top, about 3 minutes. Flip cake over and cook 2 minutes. Serve immediately with Orange-Almond Syrup, and garnish with orange segments.

Orange-Almond Syrup

1 cup orange juice
1 cinnamon stick
½ cup light maple syrup
¼ cup reserved roasted almonds

Simmer orange juice and cinnamon stick in small saucepot over medium heat until reduced to ½ cup, about 15 minutes. Add maple syrup. Remove cinnamon stick, stir in reserved roasted almonds and serve warm.

Recipe courtesy of the Florida Department of Citrus and Chef Michel Nischan.

Photo by Gary Quirling.

LANDSCAPE HIGHLIGHTS

- Evergreen in warmer zones
- Potted for container gardening
- Fragrant white flowers, colorful fruit

EDIBLE HIGHLIGHTS

- Fresh fruit from the tree
- Juiced for drinks or syrup
- Cooked as marmalade

WHERE THEY GROW BEST

- In frost-free or nearly frost-free zones with dry heat, southern coastal regions
- In full sun, but protected from scorching if grown in containers
- In fertile medium loam that drains well

HOW TO GROW THEM

- With best local characteristics (see Resources section for Agricultural Extension information)
- Hand-pollinated with small paintbrush if taken indoors during winter
- Fed with blooming solution to stimulate fruit production, especially when potted
- With plenty of water
- Pruned to eliminate old wood and crossing branches and to stimulate fruit production
- On dwarf rootstock (for potted oranges only)

SOUR ORANGES

The deciduous trifoliate orange or sour orange (*Poncirus trifoliata*) can tolerate more frost than standard citrus, surviving even to 0 degrees F in sheltered locations. This plant provides rootstock for the hardier new citrus varieties and has its own charms. Densely contorted branches are covered with long, curved thorns, so this plant makes an excellent natural security system and can be grown as a hedge, a veritable wall. It is handsome, too, with evergreen limbs even when the leaves have fallen, and lovely white flowers in spring.

The small, hard green fruits of some varieties can be made into marmalade.

Olive

Plant an olive tree and it may survive for five hundred years. Chop it down and it comes back. One reputable account tells of Mediterranean olive trees still bearing fruit after 1,500 years.

Such longevity should come as no surprise; olive trees have

figured in human affairs for at least eight thousand years. The oil pressed from harvested olives holds an esteemed place in some religions, and it gets high marks for its health properties and flavor.

Thomas Jefferson called the olive tree "the richest gift of heaven." He was a pioneer, along with Benjamin Franklin, in growing olives outside their natural "comfort zone" of dry heat and thin soil. These early Americans found that while the olive can survive in some cold climates, it won't bear fruit.

The olive tree has a beautiful form: gnarled branches covered in feathery evergreen foliage of silvery grey-green, masses of creamy white flowers, and fruits that can be pickled or pressed.

For its ornamental value alone—as an accent against a wall or in a courtyard, or standing alone on a hillside—the olive tree deserves a closer look by edible landscape gardeners throughout North America.

Like citrus trees, olives can grow in containers and be taken indoors for the winter. And because they tolerate not just poor soil, but alkaline or even salty soil, olives can grow well near the beach.

The tree itself can tolerate cold to 15 degrees F, but ripening fruit is damaged below 28 degrees F, and blossoms suffer from frost.

This fragility may not be a bad thing for cold-weather gardeners who want to experiment. Allowed to over-bear, the olive tree drops enough fruit to stain pavement and lawns, and truly, processing the fruit is a challenge.

That was the case when my family moved from the Central Valley to Southern California during my childhood. Our new yard held an olive tree between the front window and the driveway. It was lovely, but to my parents the prospect of messy olives dropping on our clean driveway was unacceptable. The olives were to get rid of, not to eat.

For "prune-a-holics" like me, who like nothing better than shaping a young tree, the olive makes a perfect project.

Olive trees demand pruning—at least when fruit is desired. Left alone, an olive tree can grow fifty feet high, thirty feet wide. But commercial growers keep their trees to twenty feet. In containers, olive trees usually grow to just ten feet.

This page and opposite: Dusk gives a pink burnish to an olive branch heavy with fruit. Olive trees were an early, but unsuccessful, experiment of early American settlers. Photos by Lillian Machado Dickson of Dickson Napa Ranch.

An olive tree can live and produce fruit for a thousand years or more, marking boundaries and creating landmarks for the generations. Photo © iStockPhoto/ Ann Murie.

They can be left in their naturally bushy habit or trained young to have spreading lower branches of great character.

Letting an olive tree bear fruit without pruning it will likely result in excess fruit, which in turn leads to smaller fruit and such stress on the tree that it can only bear in alternate years. Even a 1 percent fruit set is considered a heavy crop that should be thinned. In optimum conditions the yield can be well over one hundred pounds per tree; withholding moisture dampens the yield without killing the tree.

In the Mediterranean region, most fruit is pressed for oil. In the United States olives have been grown since the 1700s, beginning in San Diego, and most become table olives. The untreated fruit contains bitter compounds that must be leached or pickled out before the olives are edible. Although the process is laborious, olive oil may be pressed at home, and hobby presses and instructions are widely available through the Internet.

For table olives, fruit is generally, but not always, picked in the green or "straw" state before it fully ripens to purple-black. The fruit is fragile and easily bruised.

Once cured, olives are delightful as snacks, with cocktails, and in various salads and cooked foods. I especially like pieces of pitted, salt-cured olives baked into pizza dough.

LANDSCAPE HIGHLIGHTS

- Structural interest from gnarled trunks and limbs
- Attractive grey-green foliage year-round
- Attains great age
- Potted for container gardening

EDIBLE HIGHLIGHTS

- Cured olives
- Pressed for oil

WHERE IT GROWS BEST

- In hot, dry zones with long growing season for fruit, but can survive to 15 degrees F; any frost damages fruit
- In coastal regions with maximum winter temperatures around 50 degrees F
- In large containers for indoor or small-space gardening
- In thin or gritty soil with good drainage, or in clay loam
- In full sun

HOW TO GROW IT

- As a pest-free small evergreen tree
- With soil analysis to correct any leaf discoloration
- Pruned consistently to prevent excess, undersize fruit, and broken limbs
- Watered lightly except for fruit development
- To mark a distant property line
- Beyond a patio to extend visual interest

Pomegranate

Pomegranate represents adventure for me: once, age seven or eight, as I first rode my bike to streets beyond my own, I came across an unfamiliar bushy plant in front of a house that had burned down. All around it was scorched black, even the sidewalk, but there stood that bright green shrub covered with leathery dark-pink fruits: pomegranate.

I already knew pomegranates as a dessert, the skin stuffed with hundreds of juicy, garnet-colored kernels. They were sweet, with a lemony twist and plenty of crunch.

Photo © iStockPhoto/Mamarama.

In the years since, the pomegranate has become a supermarket staple and is well known in juice form for its healthful qualities, primarily high vitamin C and antioxidant content. Pomegranate kernels—berries, or "arils," actually—are used in Middle Eastern and modern American cuisine. The juice makes good jelly, and when boiled down to syrup or "molasses" it is delicious in beverages or sauces, or as a glaze for grilled meats.

As part of the edible landscape, this native of the Himalayan highlands grows in a wide range of climates, but does best—producing abundant bright red flowers and that incomparable fruit—in hot, dry regions.

The ancient pomegranate had migrated over the ages throughout the Middle East and Mediterranean regions before crossing the Atlantic with Spanish missionaries and English colonists. Pomegranates thrived in California, but did less well in New England and the South; they would not bear fruit in cold or humid conditions, although the vegetation could survive. Technically the roots live to 10 degrees F, while the branches may die back below 20 degrees.

I have faithfully replicated the early Americans' experiments in my own North Carolina garden. Planted in the driest corner of my garden and with twenty-five pounds of added sand apiece to replicate Morocco, my two pomegranates are happy through the summer months, their limbs clothed in glossy, red-edged leaves; but so far, they haven't flowered or set fruit. In truth, my climate may be too cold for that, but I still enjoy the glossy foliage as contrast to the rougher plants.

The pomegranate blossom, with its hot-pink petals unfurling, gives the edible landscape a blast of color. ©iStock-Photos/Laticia Ragle.

Pomegranate Syrup and Pomegranate Molasses

Recipes for pomegranate syrup and the thicker "molasses" differ mainly in the amount of time required to simmer the juice—with sugar and citrus—to the desired consistency.

The amount of sugar in relation to raw juice varies widely according to the source. For every 4 cups of extracted juice, add as little as ½ cup or as much as 2½ cups sugar. Likewise, lemon juice varies from 1 tablespoon to ¼ cup per 4 cups of juice, according to taste. Batches may be up to 8 cups of juice at a time (beginning with 10 cups, minus 2 cups of sediment).

Combine all ingredients in an enameled kettle; heat slowly until sugar dissolves. Simmer 50 to 60 minutes for syrup, 70 to 90 minutes for molasses. Volume should reduce by a third for syrup, a half for molasses.

Cool and store in jars in the refrigerator, or process in a boiling water bath to seal.

Juice made from fresh pomegranates is rich in antioxidants and can be bottled for year-round enjoyment. Photo by Henry Firus of Flagstaffotos, Australia.

The deciduous, pest-free pomegranate has several uses in garden design.

Planted in a row, pomegranate bushes can be allowed to follow their natural suckering habit and maintained as a hedge. Or they can be used as specimen plants, gaining their full twenty-foot height.

Commonly, though, they are pruned of suckers and kept to eight or ten feet for maximum fruit. Although the pomegranate is drought resistant, it needs regular water for fruit production.

Pomegranate is a member of the rose family and is related to the apple. Its Latin name, *Punica granatum*, contains a lot of information: "Punic" relates to the plant's spread under the Phoenicians, while "pom" and "granatum" together roughly mean "seeded apple."

Pomegranate fruit is simultaneously bothersome and exciting. Once the outer skin has been removed, there's still an unappealing yellowish membrane to penetrate. Only then are the beautiful and delicious arils released; many cooks like to separate these colorful and stain-producing nuggets in a sink filled with water to minimize the mess.

The berries, seeds and all, can be eaten as is or wrung inside a moistened towel to release the juice. Another method is to roll the whole fruit until it softens, then puncture the skin and keep squeezing.

When using the juice for jelly, syrup, or molasses, let it sit overnight or longer in the refrigerator so that the sediment can settle before processing. The result will be clear, rather than cloudy, products.

LANDSCAPE HIGHLIGHTS

- Intense red blossoms
- Glossy summer foliage

EDIBLE HIGHLIGHTS

- Fresh fruit from the bush
- Juiced for beverages, juice, or jelly

WHERE IT GROWS BEST

- In dry climates
- In full sun
- In light, well-drained soil

HOW TO GROW IT

- As a deciduous shrub to fifteen feet tall and spreading
- Pruned of suckers for fruit production
- Massed, unpruned, as a hedge
- Watered lightly except for fruit development
- With underplantings of lacy white or blue flowers, like love-in-a-mist
- Near a water source for easy irrigation during fruit set

WHERE TO FIND POME-GRANATE BUSHES

Residents of the far West or deep South are more likely than most gardeners to find pomegranate plants at a local nursery or garden center. Others will need to order by mail; consult a local agricultural agent (see Resources section) for recommendations about reputable nurseries.

Cross-pollination is not necessary but will increase fruit set. Recommended varieties are 'Wonderful' and 'Favorite', and dwarf varieties are available.

Once established, pomegranates can be easily propagated from hardwood cuttings in soil.

Photo by Nan K. Chase.

Wildflowers

They're everywhere!

Wildflowers are widespread native plants that flourish on their own, beautiful and productive without the human touch. Wildflowers circle the globe, providing food for people, birds, mammals, and insects. They grow an inch high, a foot high, thirty feet high, with mind-boggling variety in color, form, and habit.

Having survived millions of years of genetic adaptation on Earth, wildflowers are the easiest components to grow in the edible landscape. They have few pests or diseases, and little need for pruning or special care.

American native plants and their offspring add so much to the edible landscape because wildflowers take so many forms: trees, shrubs, flowering masses, even cacti.

Although each wildflower occupies a specialized niche, many share the valuable characteristic of multi-season appeal. Blooming wild roses look good in spring and summer, for instance, but they also have brilliant fall color and continuing interest through winter, when the last ripe red hips glisten with frost.

Many wildflowers offer delicious fruit in season, the freshest food imaginable, rich in flavor and nutrition. It's natural and organic, essentially harvested from the wild.

A wildflower in its ideal habitat always looks healthy, and the wonder of wildflowers is how they span vast geographical regions across North America. The same plant can grow in habitats as diverse as Quebec and Florida. Take the humble yucca, with its edible flowers, fruits, and roots: it lives in the western deserts, the frigid upper Plains states, and the moist Appalachian Mountains.

The secret to using wildflowers in the edible landscape is to duplicate their natural habitats.

Pawpaw and persimmon trees want the complex leaf litter and dappled shade of the forest margins; they grow best when used as understory plants beneath the cover of mature hardwoods.

Wild roses and sunflowers can survive over a wide range of temperatures and sunlight conditions, but they must have air circulation and adequate water.

Yucca and prickly pear mustn't sit in water. They don't care how hot or cold they get as long as the soil drains well and there's plenty of sun.

I have found great joy, in my own edible landscape, from fitting all of these plants into half a dozen microclimates: shady areas with well-composted soil, airy perennial borders around the lawn, and dry, thin soil in patches of intense sun.

In selecting the plants to include in this section I have had to leave out many interesting candidates. My criteria included the possible range of cultivation, the degree of potential invasiveness in the landscape, the degree of beauty through the year, ease and quantity of harvest, and ease of food preparation.

So I concentrate on just five groupings: pawpaw, persimmon, wild roses, sunflowers, and the yucca and prickly pear together—all wonderful in the edible landscape. It's hard to choose a favorite.

The tougher the plant, it seems, the more tender and lovely the flower. Both prickly pear flowers (left) and yucca blossoms (below left) are delicate delights. Photos by Nan K. Chase.

Pawpaw

"It was love at first bite," says North Carolina horticulturist and pawpaw grower Derek Morris of the pawpaw fruit. He grows an amazing twenty-nine varieties of pawpaw in his nearly one-acre yard in Winston-Salem. "Simply put, it was the most delicious fruit I had ever tasted, and the creamy, smooth texture was an instant hit with me.

"I couldn't believe that this fruit was not found in every grocery store and that it was not as common as the banana or apple."

Pawpaw nourished the Native American peoples, and then colonial settlers discovered its delicious, creamy fruit. The foliage turns golden in fall. Photo by Scott Bauer, United States Department of Agriculture.

There are reasons the pawpaw is not better known: the custard-like ripe fruit is simply too delicate to handle and ship much distance, and it doesn't store well once off the tree. And the pawpaw began to lose habitat with rampant suburban development.

But researchers are confident that the storied pawpaw is on the verge of a big revival and will soon become a feature in the edible yard. Already some growers in the Southeast have begun planting orchards and expect to be supplying local buyers soon.

Pawpaw Ice Cream "Derek Morris"

3 cups milk

3 cups cream

3 cups sugar

3 lemons or 2 oranges (optional)

2 cups mashed pawpaw pulp, seeds removed

Mix together milk, cream, and sugar. Place in ice cream maker and turn until mushy. Add juice from citrus, if using, and pawpaw pulp. Proceed until frozen.

This ice cream is delicious with or without the citrus juice.

Recipe courtesy of Derek Morris.

The graceful, small pawpaw tree—growing to thirty feet—not only furnishes delightful fruit, but its oversize leaves provide open shade in summer and excellent yellow leaves in fall. Despite its mature size, pawpaw is considered a wildflower for its flowering habit and widely naturalized spread.

As the only place the zebra swallowtail butterfly lays eggs and where its caterpillars eat after hatching, the pawpaw tree attracts these stunning creatures as a bonus.

There are towns named Paw Paw in West Virginia and Kentucky, Michigan, and Oklahoma, with townships of the same name scattered throughout the Ohio River Valley (the spelling of pawpaw appears many different ways). Today, one breeder of pawpaws names his plant lines after river systems of the East: Shenandoah, Potomac, Susquehanna, Rappahannock, Allegheny, and Wabash.

Those moist, shady, well-drained lowlands provide the perfect shelter for pawpaw trees, which spread as thickets. They prefer a slightly acid soil and are one of the only plants—along with persimmon—that can grow well near black walnut trees.

As the northernmost New World branch of the large, mostly tropical, custard apple family, the pawpaw, *Asimina triloba*, can

Good to the last spoonful, pawpaw fruit tastes a bit like mango and banana. Photo by R. Dennis Hager, courtesy of R. Neal Peterson.

certainly survive the cracking cold winters of central North America. Its bell-shaped brown flower in spring presents an intricate composition in layers of three: like a thick trillium blossom curled back on itself. While interesting, the flower is relatively small and considered inconspicuous.

Pawpaws figured prominently in early American folklore and were known as important food for all kinds of wildlife. George Washington liked to eat chilled pawpaw fruit—according to various tales—as did Daniel Boone and Mark Twain. The Native American people ate them, and so did the Lewis and Clark explorers.

The pudding-like pawpaw fruit (sometimes called false-banana, Hoosier banana, or poor man's banana) is described as an entrancing mixture of light tropical flavors with caramel or butterscotch overtones: mango, pineapple, banana, avocado, peaches, pears. This complex flavor develops only after the first frosts of the season, so pawpaw is a late-season treat that ripens on the tree.

Vitamin-rich pawpaw fruits can weigh up to a pound apiece; the bean-shaped pods are several inches or more long. Cooks find the pulp freezes well or can be baked into pies and breads. Pawpaw can also be dried.

To grow pawpaws, it's important to understand the young trees' need for shade protection and adequate moisture. Derek Morris and others have found the pawpaw a challenge to get started, given its long taproot and a web of delicate side roots.

A family heirloom, this pawpaw tree in southern Illinois shows off masses of bright golden fall foliage. Photo by Rhonda Ashby Coulter.

They suggest working with established pawpaw breeders, using containerized rather than bare root plants if possible, and mulching well to keep the young roots cool and damp. Mature trees bear larger fruit in full sun, so be patient until all conditions occur.

That's just what I'm doing with my two small pawpaws—different varieties for required cross-pollination—as they get established in the shade of my shagbark hickory.

LANDSCAPE HIGHLIGHTS
- Cold-hardy small tree
- Golden fall foliage
- Zebra swallowtail butterfly habitat

EDIBLE HIGHLIGHTS
- Fresh fruit from the tree
- Baked into bread or pudding
- Frozen for year-round use

WHERE THEY GROW BEST
- In dappled shade, forest understory
- In well-drained soil rich in organic matter
- In humid climates with cold winters

HOW TO GROW THEM
- With trees planted young
- so long taproot grows undisturbed
- With other varieties for cross-pollination
- For fall fruit as frost occurs
- In a small yard, as an anchor plant that won't grow too large
- Near a patio for pleasant shade and visual interest

Persimmon

When I was a girl in Fresno, we had a failing-to-thrive persimmon tree in our small front yard. It bore one persimmon every year—I remember its velvety burnt-orange mass—and every year my mother baked one batch of persimmon cookies. They were large cookies the color of faded

Persimmons are difficult to ship, since they ripen best on the tree. After frost comes, the flavors deepen and take on spicy overtones. Photo © iStockPhoto/Impact-image.

pumpkins, with a creamy-crumbly texture I liked.

So maybe it was nostalgia that led me to plant my own persimmon tree a few years back, although the tree's natural beauty and wonderful fruit naturally make it a contender in the edible landscape. My tree is coming along nicely, in a sloping bed with half a day's shade.

The persimmon—the native American species—shares many characteristics with the pawpaw: both have gorgeous yellow leaves in fall, both are small trees that live in moist woodlands,

Persimmon Puddin'

3 tablespoons butter

2 cups raw persimmon pulp

3 beaten eggs

2 cups flour

1/2 teaspoon soda

1/2 teaspoon salt

1 3/4 cups sugar

1 teaspoon cinnamon

1 teaspoon nutmeg

1 1/2 cups milk

Melt butter in a shallow baking dish. In a mixing bowl, blend pulp with beaten eggs. Mix dry ingredients together in a separate mixing bowl; then add dry ingredients alternately with milk to persimmon mixture. Pour into baking dish with melted butter. Bake at 300 degrees F for about 1 hour.

Reprinted with permission from Southern Appalachian Mountain Cookin': Authentic Ol' Mountain Family Recipes, ©2004, APS, Inc.

Persimmon Bread

1 cup sugar

1 1/2 sticks butter (12 tablespoons), softened

2 eggs, beaten

2 cups flour, sifted

1/2 teaspoon baking soda

Dash salt

1/2 cup chopped nuts, such as walnuts or pecans

1 cup persimmon pulp

Heat oven to 325 degrees F. Line loaf pan with waxed paper.

Cream sugar and butter until light and fluffy. Add eggs, flour, baking soda, salt, nuts, and persimmon pulp until combined.

Bake 70 minutes, just until a toothpick inserted in center comes out clean.

Recipe courtesy of Derek Morris.

both have long taproots that make them difficult to transplant except when young, and both have fruit that's considered a delicacy but is difficult to pack and ship. Like the pawpaw, persimmon is a flowering plant that spreads without cultivation, thus a wildflower.

There are two main kinds of persimmons generally considered too astringent to eat until fully ripened: the Asian persimmons, *Diospyros kaki,* and the American persimmons, *D. virginiana.* Additionally, non-astringent Asian varieties, with crunchy rather than jellified innards, can be sliced and eaten without waiting.

Asian persimmons grow smaller—twelve feet or so—and are less cold-hardy than American persimmons. Their main advantage comes in the fruit, which can be picked half-ripened and left to finish off the tree; the seedless fruit is processed more easily.

American persimmons grow to fifty feet or more, although they are commonly pruned lower, and they can survive temperatures to -25 degrees F. The fruit has seeds and must ripen completely on the tree, which usually requires heavy frost. Then the delicious pulp carries overtones of cinnamon and allspice, or as pawpaw and persimmon grower Derek Morris describes it, "Pumpkin mixed with honey and plum" or "wet, spicy apricot."

Hybrid species have been developed in Russia blending desirable characteristics of Asian and American persimmons, and Texas persimmon, *D. texana,* also bears edible fruit and has distinctive scaling bark.

All are members of the ebony family, with extremely hard wood used historically for high impact situations: golf "woods," billiard cues, and, when there was still an American textile industry, shuttles for looms.

The thick bark of the American persimmon, whose natural range is the eastern United States south of Pennsylvania, has a pleasing incised "block" pattern. The trees are not fussy about soil, and they thrive along roadsides and on waste ground. Fragrant white springtime flowers grace the branches.

Tannins make persimmon fruit challenging to use. Unripe, the fruits are bitter and disagreeable. Ripe and freed from these acids' effects, the sweet, soft pulp can be used a number of ways: dried, frozen, and, most commonly, baked into puddings and breads.

North Carolina horticulturist Derek Morris, who grows many pawpaw trees in his yard, also raises some twenty persimmons. He eats the pulp right from the skin.

Persimmons appear on the holiday table in the form of bread, pudding, or even a garnish for poultry or meat. Photo by Marcus Nilsson.

LANDSCAPE HIGHLIGHTS
- Golden fall foliage
- Winter wildlife food source

EDIBLE HIGHLIGHTS
- Flavorful fresh or cold-ripened fruit
- Baked into pudding or bread

WHERE THEY GROW BEST
- In dappled shade or full sun
- In fertile, well-drained soil
- In climates with frost

HOW TO GROW THEM
- With trees planted young so long taproot grows undisturbed
- For fall fruit as frost occurs
- As focal point for fall and winter interest
- Spaced 10–12 feet apart
- With small spring bulbs around them

WHAT KIND OF PERSIMMON?

American persimmons are more cold-hardy, surviving to -25 degrees F, Zone 4, while Asian persimmons do well to about 0 degrees F, Zone 7. Less well-known Ukrainian persimmons are hybrids of the two.

The American persimmon varieties grow taller than Asian varieties, as tall as thirty feet compared to about twelve feet. The fruit ripening habit is different too. American persimmons are generally too bitter to eat until fully ripe on the tree, while most Asian persimmons can be picked half ripe to finish ripening later.

Prickly Pear, Yucca

Nothing says "Keep Out!" like a big prickly pear cactus, but yucca comes close.

I love these plants in the edible landscape for their year-round character and color, their toughness in any climate, and their surprising beauty.

Both yucca, commonly *Yucca filamentosa,* and prickly pear

Prickly pear cactus exhibits an astonishing range of colors and shapes during the year. By fall, deep pink edible "pears" have replaced the yellow flowers. Photo by Nan K. Chase.

species of the genus *Opuntia* grow well from the Southwest to New England to the Dakotas, adding architectural grandeur and a sense of security.

They offer year-round appeal: soft new growth and gorgeous flowers in spring, vigorous texture in summer, unusual fruits in fall, and a place for snow to rest sculpturally in winter.

And while it may come as news, both yucca and prickly pear have delicious edible parts.

Yucca has a strong tuberous taproot and multiplies steadily but not uncontrollably. Its crown of tough foliage is softened by curly filaments along the edges of each spine.

It is perfect as a two-foot-high ground cover in garden wastelands. In my yard, yucca occupies the dusty heights above

Grilled or Broiled Yucca with Huancaina Sauce

Wash and peel several large yucca roots. Slice lengthwise and extract the fibrous core. Cut roots into finger-size pieces, cover with water in a saucepan, bring to the boil with salt, and simmer 30 minutes, or until just firm. Drain.

Brush with vegetable oil and broil or grill until golden and sizzling, about 3–4 minutes per side, watching carefully to prevent burning. Serve immediately with Huancaina sauce for dipping.

Countless versions of Huancaina sauce call for 2–3 fresh, seeded aji chilies, chopped coarsely and sautéed with onions and garlic and then added to a blender with a cup or more of mild white cheese and up to a cup of milk, with added oil to produce a thick, creamy consistency.

several tall rock walls where nothing else takes hold.

I have found it easy to transplant yucca and begin new beds. All it takes is a deep hole and one big drink of water to get acclimated; after that the yuccas are carefree.

Once established, in a few years, the blossoms begin. And they are spectacular: five-foot-tall spears that rise from the ground, phallus-like, and spring open like Christmas trees decked with heavy, waxy, bell-shaped blooms. This is gardening with style!

A friend from Mexico craves these blossoms, for the petals and unopened buds are delicious fresh in salads or sauteed in oil with onions, garlic, and chilies to make relish. Later in the season, the ripe fruits (drooping fleshy pods) are also edible, although many gardeners trim the spent flower stalks before that.

I like cooked yucca root, especially when it's prepared by an expert Peruvian chef like the one at La Canela in Rockville, Maryland. There my parents and I recently enjoyed fried yuccas with Huancaina sauce—feather-light golden slices with a smooth, fiery sauce—and "yuquitas"—balls of mashed yucca stuffed with crabmeat, baked, and served with tomato sauce.

Prickly pear cactuses—a group of similar species—present the greatest contradictions in gardening.

The flowers can stop you in your tracks with their diaphanous layers of yellow or pink, packed against spring's light-green vegetation; they remind me of ballet dancers' twirling skirts turned upside down, or sea anemones.

The egg-size mature fruits, called "tunas" in Spanish, have their own kind of rough beauty, appearing as clumps of pink-red pears that glow from an iridescent under-layer. The fluffy pastel interior tastes like candy; and the experience of eating it is accentuated by the large, crunchy black seeds known in folklore for their beneficial heart and blood properties.

Even the flat, paddle-like leaves, called "nopales" (no-PAHL-es), are edible, once the spines are removed, and have long formed an important part of the indigenous Southwest diet.

But handling prickly pear cactus can be terribly painful (thus their utility as security fencing, whereas the yucca only looks fierce). The short spines seem to seek out any bit of unprotected skin, and they are slender and difficult to remove; it can take weeks for one to work its way out.

A practiced hand can quickly cut out the spines from a nopal, and then it's ready to cook, broiled or boiled for salads or stews. That same hand can also slice open a ripe tuna to extract the pulp. But until you have mastered the art of handling prickly pears bare-handed—and I have watched it—wear gloves and use tongs.

With those warnings, go ahead and add prickly pear to the edible landscape. You will always see beauty and nourishment where others might only see cactus.

LANDSCAPE HIGHLIGHTS
- Evergreen screening, security
- Spring, summer flowers
- Cold-hardy, winter interest with snow
- Bright pink prickly pears in winter

EDIBLE HIGHLIGHTS
- Yucca flowers and buds in sauces, salads
- Yucca root fried or baked
- Prickly pear fruits and de-spined paddles

WHERE THEY GROW BEST
- In full sun, although yucca can grow in cooler, moist conditions
- In thin, sandy or poor soil with occasional rain or watering
- Along walls or on terraces where water drains quickly

HOW TO GROW THEM
- Planting yuccas from young divisions of the long taproot; dig deep hole, fill with water, tamp soil around plant
- Planting prickly pear stem cuttings from paddles in shallow sand, moistening and firming plants in place as gradually spreading wildflowers taking several seasons to flower and bear fruit
- With lacy or vining plants like nasturtium
- Near liatris or other spiked plants

Rose

The rose is a botanical mothership with connections to much of what grows in our gardens: everything from nectarines to strawberries.

"Queen of flowers!" one source exclaims.

Roses have universal appeal for the intense perfume and

The white Rugosa rose brightens the edible landscape with lovely flowers in spring and summer, before the hips turn red in fall. Photo courtesy of David Austin Roses.

entrancing beauty of their flowers. They also help pollination among other plants.

There are wild roses native to North America, or introduced and naturalized, which are adaptable from seaside to mountaintop. And there are hybridized roses, with thoroughbred refinement, suitable only where the climate cooperates and people can pamper them.

Wild roses, to make the situation more complicated, can be quite good in the garden—or highly destructive.

Let's agree to cheat and consider several native North American roses and several imported roses together (imported, that is, during colonial times or earlier and then spreading) before choosing the most useful and least intrusive for the edible landscape.

First, a word about why roses should be considered edible at all.

For one thing, rose petals have a light, sweet flavor and can be eaten fresh in salads, where they add unexpected color; one writer pairs them with cucumbers for a visual treat. The young shoots of some roses, carefully cleaned, are also edible, with a pleasant crunch.

It is the rose's fruit that merits attention and that has a long, nutritionally important role in civilization, especially in northern climates where other fruits are difficult to grow, and during wartime, when sources of vitamin C are interrupted.

The small fruits called rose hips have the highest vitamin C content of any fresh food, and while they can be eaten raw, more commonly rose hips are cooked before use. The seeds, which are hairy and give bad tickles to the throat, are almost always either cooked and strained out or just spit out. Rose hips can be processed—strained for juice—to make jelly, syrup, and sauces. That goodness can be bottled and kept all year. Rose hips and rose petals also produce specialty wines, cordials, and liqueurs.

Hips are pulpy, seed-filled pods, which in late fall grace rose bushes with their red or orange colors (even dark blue). The hips vary in size and shape, usually not much larger than a grape. Covered in frost in a landscape otherwise drained of color, they make a spectacular display.

Unlike the more demanding hybrid roses, wild roses have spent tens of millions of years adapting to local conditions. They are nearly disease free and pest free. They require little pruning or fertilizing, can withstand temperatures well below zero, and can grow in poor soils.

In some cases, wild roses grow to ten or fifteen feet high, forming impressive hedges. In all cases, before planting wild roses check with local agricultural officials to see if your choice is even legal—some wild roses are considered noxious and are banned. Of genus *Rosa* the main offenders are multiflora roses, including Cherokee rose (ironically, not a true native). Don't plant these.

Do investigate other species of *Rosa* for what they can add to your own edible landscape: dog rose, prairie rose, Carolina rose, glauca rose, nootka rose (a western native), and countless crossbred native roses.

My favorite is *R. rugosa*, the wrinkled rose. I love its highly textural green leaves and its intoxicating pink flowers.

Rose Hip Sauce for Meat

2 cups rose hips, seeded
1 1/2 cups water
1/2 cup sugar
3 tablespoons cornstarch
1/2 cup white wine (optional)

Simmer the rose hips in the water for 1 hour. Add the sugar and cook for 5 more minutes. Add the cornstarch and continue simmering for 3 minutes, stirring constantly. Add the white wine just before serving, if desired.

Reprinted from A Taste of Heritage: Crow Indian Recipes and Herbal Medicines *by Alma Hogan Snell by permission of the University of Nebraska Press. ©2006 by Alma Hogan Snell.*

Rose Hip Jelly

This is best made after the first frost. Pick about a pound of rose hips; cut off the blossom. Barely cover with water and simmer until fruit is very soft. Use a jelly bag to extract juice. Add a box of pectin, bring to a high boil quickly, add an amount of sugar equal to amount of juice. Bring to a high boil and hold for one minute. Stir and skim. Pour into sterilized jars and cover with paraffin.

(Author's note: Jars may be sealed in a conventional boiling water bath instead of with paraffin.)

Reprinted with permission from Southern Appalachian Mountain Cookin': Authentic Ol' Mountain Family Recipes, *©2004, APS, Inc.*

Rose hips, with their concentrated vitamin C, stay on the bush late in the fall. Preserved as jelly, they can supply important nutrients during winter. Photo courtesy of David Austin Roses.

LANDSCAPE HIGHLIGHTS

- Enhances spring pollination throughout garden
- Summer blooms and fragrance
- Fall leaf color
- Winter color from ripe "hips"

EDIBLE HIGHLIGHTS

- Hips cooked as nutritious syrup or jelly
- Cooked in sauces
- For herbal tea

WHERE IT GROWS BEST

- In almost any climate or region, depending on species; some to -40 degrees F, Zone 3
- In full sun
- In porous, slightly acidic soil

HOW TO GROW IT

- Check with local Agricultural Extension service (see Resources section) for best wild varieties and for any warnings about banned invasive roses
- Keep plants weed free, with good air circulation through canes
- In well-prepared beds, with ample fertilizer and water
- Massed as hedges or singly as specimens
- Near garden statuary, rail fence, or boulders for visual contrast
- Spectacular against variegated yucca

WHAT KIND TO GROW?

First, before choosing any rose for the edible landscape, find out about invasive rose alerts in your area. Roses are beneficial, but not all roses are good neighbors.

For plentiful rose hips try *Rosa rugosa,* the spreading "wrinkled" rose, or *R. canina,* the dog rose; some gardeners like the Moyes rose, *R. moyesii,* or the cinnamon rose, *R. majalis.* These plants require little care and can thrive in various conditions.

Fussier tea roses, while lovely and often fragrant, involve more care: regular pruning and fertilizing, and frequent watering while blooming. They are more susceptible to diseases and insect pests, which require treatment.

Some suppliers specialize in heirloom roses, which combine beauty and vigor, and they will ship top-quality specimens.

Sunflower

Put aside, just now, images of gigantic seed-studded disks of sunflowers towering overhead.

Ponder instead the more delicate charms of wild sunflowers, of which there are as many as one hundred species in the genus *Helianthus*.

Jerusalem artichoke, a wild sunflower, has nutritious tuberous roots with a nutty flavor and which can be enjoyed raw or cooked. Photo by Paul Fenwick, Coburg, Victoria, Australia.

Most of them are tall, most bloom in shades of yellow, and all add late-summer interest to the edible landscape while attracting birds and insects until frost comes. Beyond that, diversity reigns.

Many of the wild sunflowers are perennial, returning year after year in greater profusion, while others grow as annuals from seed. Native species have adapted to every part of the country and can flourish in shade, swampy ground, or dry soil.

With their open structure of long stems and large or lacy leaves adorned with wide-eyed blooms, sunflowers coexist well in mixtures with other flowering plants lower down. In that

Birds and bees love the hybridized sunflower just as much people do, so it's important to protect ripening seed heads from hungry garden visitors. Photo by Nan K. Chase.

way, sunflowers add texture to the garden without actually taking up much space.

Early North American inhabitants learned that sunflowers meant food. The seeds provided protein-rich flour and meal, and oil for cooking. The petals were sometimes cooked too, and there was one especially delicious sunflower food: Jerusalem artichoke, *H. tuberosus.*

There's still good reason to enjoy the tuberous roots of that plant as they are harvested during fall, winter, and springtime. The roots are about the size of fingerling potatoes and can be eaten raw, boiled, roasted, or fried.

High in potassium and iron, Jerusalem artichokes taste fantastic and are easy to prepare. And once they get established in the garden they will produce great quantities of tubers—virtually free food.

Nan's Salty-Roasted Sunflower Seeds

Harvest ripe heads of Mammoth Russian or Russian Giant sunflower as they begin to dry but before birds eat the seeds. Continue air-drying the heads indoors on paper until seeds (actually the seed husks) are completely dry; then rub individual seeds from the flower disk.

Rinse seeds in water to remove dust, and soak overnight in salt brine—½ cup salt to 4 cups boiling water. Drain.

Bake at low temperature (180 degrees F) on cookie sheets or in baking pans, 2 to 3 hours, turning seeds every half hour to ensure even baking. Do not overcook.

Cool and store in clean jars.

To eat raw as a snack, simply brush and rinse all the dirt off, rather than peeling, since nutrients are concentrated near the skin. Slice the roots thin; the taste is like a sweet, fine-grained water chestnut.

Pan fried in a little oil, chunks of Jerusalem artichoke puff up and turn crispy brown—wonderful with catsup. The tubers can also be boiled and then mashed, or they can be oven roasted with olive oil and fresh herbs.

Jerusalem artichokes are sometimes called sunchokes and sold in the grocery store. They are not related to real artichokes, but have come by the name by linguistic accident.

The Jerusalem artichoke's only drawback as a garden plant is its tendency to reproduce widely if not controlled. Nonetheless, the flat, spreading flower petals and distinctive rounded seed heads reaching ten feet tall make a bold statement en masse.

In my volunteer work at the Daniel Boone Native Gardens in Boone, North Carolina, I have come to know and love several sunflower species that thrive in the Appalachian Mountains.

There's the giant sunflower, *H. giganteus,* which is not to be confused with the Mammoth Russian or Russian Giant varieties of the common sunflower, *H. annuus.* The giant sunflower earned its name not from giant flowers, but from its giant height, often 12 feet or more; the flowers are of modest size.

Maximilian's Sunflower, *H. maximilianii,* has handsome dark brown stems to set off its golden flowers. Like the giant sunflower, it is perennial.

My favorite is the perennial woodland sunflower, which defies stereotype by living in damp, dark woodlands. The broad leaves produce layers of greenery in the woods, against which the brilliant mid-yellow flowers look especially lovely.

Other sunflowers: cucumberleaf and silverleaf sunflowers, both annuals; the well-named showy sunflower; and the willowleaf sunflower, to name a few.

Finally, to those big familiar disks of color, the hybridized sunflowers that produce lots and lots of pretty seeds that we love to eat. They are easy to grow and highly productive per square inch of garden space. Be sure to plant them, but consider protecting the almost ripe seed heads from birds and squirrels by tying muslin or lightweight orchard cloth around the heads.

LANDSCAPE HIGHLIGHTS
- Summer blooms
- Perennial varieties for every zone
- Annuals grow quickly from seed
- Wildlife food source

EDIBLE HIGHLIGHTS
- Raw or cooked root of Jerusalem artichoke
- Roasted seeds store well

WHERE IT GROWS BEST
- In spacious beds
- As companions to other bright, late-summer flowers, such as black-eyed Susan, New England aster, dahlia, goldenrod, or Turk's-cap lily (blue, orange, yellow)
- In drought conditions and blasting heat, or in dappled shade and moist soil, depending on species

HOW TO GROW IT
- As sod busters in poor soil
- Leaving plenty of space between plants for stalk development
- As pest-free goldfinch magnets needing little care

WHERE TO BUY SUNFLOWERS
Seed packets for the Giant Russian or Mammoth Russian varieties, which yield large seedheads full of delicious seeds, are readily available in the spring at garden centers or by mail, as are many smaller decorative varieties.

Tubers to start Jerusalem artichokes are available by the pound in the produce section of many grocery stores, although they may be labeled as "sunchokes."

As for the more unusual native sunflower species, do research in your own community to find local sources of live specimens rather than seeds if possible. Garden clubs and local nurseries can help, or you can investigate Internet sources.

Preserving the Harvest

Basics of freezing, canning, dehydrating, pressing, and fermenting

It's not enough simply to grow food in an edible landscape. As the garden matures there should be ever-larger harvests, so preserving the surplus nutrition—whether in canning jars, by dehydration, freezing, or fermentation—assures you a supply of inexpensive organic food and drink throughout the year. You know exactly what's in the food you preserve yourself!

Putting up food becomes a habit, and then a pleasure . . . and eventually a way of life. Nothing compares to your own delicious and varied harvest, lovingly prepared and preserved.

Through most of human history there was no such thing as a supermarket, nowhere to get fresh fruit in the middle of winter. Mostly, people were tied to the land and had to "put up," "put by," or otherwise preserve their seasonal harvest for the lean months.

From ancient times farmers have used the sun to dry food or used simple chemical action to turn various crops into wine (and harder stuff). Even before electricity and domestic refrigeration, homemakers prepared pickles, jams, jellies, and other delicious foods, and preserved them in crocks or jars; salt, sugar, vinegar, and spices can all act as preservatives. And since the advent of the freezer, freezing foods has been a favorite way to preserve extra produce harvested at its peak.

We may have lost some of those skills through lack of use, but fortunately they're not difficult to relearn.

Each method has advantages, and some have disadvantages. Each has its adherents. For me, nothing beats canning; a cupboard filled

with row upon row of glass jars in sparkling summer color is tremendously satisfying when the snow flies, and canned delicacies make wonderful gifts. But canning is an energy hog, and it's hot, laborious work.

Many cooks favor freezing for its convenience, but I have never adopted what one cookbook calls "good freezer habits." And in the event of a power outage, it's possible to lose a whole season's work. That doesn't happen with canning, dehydrating, or fermenting.

There's no reason to restrict yourself to only one method. In fact, many of the foods in this book lend themselves to all four ways of preserving food. The blueberry, for instance, makes tasty jam. Blueberries also freeze well, produce flavorful wine, and can even be dehydrated—carefully—to make little blueberry "raisins" for snacking or baking.

If you've never tried these methods, today is a good time to start learning. For detailed information on canning, dehydrating, or freezing foods, visit the website of the National Center for Home Food Preservation, www.uga.edu/nchfp/. For winemaking, consult any of the new or used books available on the topic.

And don't forget to use the resources of the United States Department of Agriculture's Cooperative Extension Service where you live. You may find "loaner" equipment and the services of a trained agent free of charge, or low-cost classes and workshops. When I first moved to the countryside thirty years ago, a home extension agent came to my house and guided me through the canning process step by step. Visit www.csrees.usda.gov for a locator and further information.

The diminutive crabapple packs a big, flavorful punch in the form of juice and jelly. The rosy fruits ripen in late summer and early autumn. Photo by www.rebeccadangelophotography.com.

Freezing

Freezing is a quick, easy way to preserve fresh foods, and it has the advantage of being a good way to save small batches as fruit, nuts, berries, and herbs come ripe. Nutritional values and flavors remain intact for some time, generally a year.

On the other hand, frozen foods stay in a dark, out-of-the-way place, so it's only too easy to forget about quantities of produce before the quality deteriorates. Effective freezing requires some kind of record-keeping or stacking system to assure that you use what you've put away in a timely way.

For best results, don't skimp on storage containers—buy only top-quality plastic bags and freezer boxes.

Fruit keeps more of its flavor when frozen in a sugar or honey syrup in containers—the "wet pack" method—or by "sugar pack," which mixes the fruit with unheated sugar before it is put into freezer bags or boxes. Guidelines and proportions are available online from the National Center for Home Food Preservation; see the Resources section.

Fruit and especially berries can also be frozen dry, in chunks of fruit or individually in the case of berries. These are rinsed and frozen first in a single layer on a cookie sheet, then packed into containers, making them easier to separate and use in small amounts.

Freezing nuts is favored for storage because it greatly prolongs flavor and nutritional life over storage at room temperature. Nuts may be frozen shelled or unshelled in plastic bags. Do not roast or cook nuts before freezing. Some gardeners keep nutmeats in a moist place overnight before freezing them, in order to reduce brittleness. Frozen nuts thaw quickly.

There are various ways to freeze herbs, and some herbs appear better than others after freezing even if the nutritional value is unaffected. In general, wash and pat dry herbs, and either freeze them in storage bags or freeze them first in a layer on a cookie sheet and then pack into bags. Herbs may also be mixed into a butter or olive-oil paste and frozen into ice cube trays, or they may be frozen in water in ice cube trays.

Many cooks use a vacuum sealer in conjunction with freezing

(and dehydrating). Removing air from the storage wrapping slows deterioration, increases shelf life, and reduces freezer burn. A good quality counter-top vacuum sealer with supply of reusable zipper top storage bags will be less than $100, a worthy investment in food freshness. Vacuum sealing takes just minutes.

Shelled pecans freeze well, or they can be cleaned and stored in airtight containers. Photo courtesy of the Georgia Pecan Commission.

Dehydrating

An electric dehydrator is simply a modern way to dry food. In humid climates a dehydrator is a must, while in desert air it may not be necessary at all. Some gardeners find that solar dehydrators work well.

Dehydrated foods keep most of their nutrient content, and they don't require added sugar to process, as in canning or freezing. In fact, dehydrating concentrates the natural sugars; that's why fruit leather made from fresh peaches, plums, or other orchard fruit is delicious for healthy snacking. A special tray is used inside a dehydrator to make leathers. The dehydration process removes about 80 percent of moisture content from fruit and reduces the weight.

Dried foods keep well in jars or sealed canisters, once out of the dehydrator, and when vacuum packed will keep a very long time without deterioration—perfect for camping or traveling.

The dehydrator is cheap—often less than $50 for a good quality American-made product—and so safe and easy to use that young children can help out (not like canning).

Just about any homegrown food can be dehydrated, including fruit, nuts, and herbs, in addition to meat and vegetables. Because various kinds of foods take on different characteristics in drying, be sure to follow any manufacturer's instructions for food preparation and drying times (these vary from a few hours to a day or so, depending on temperature and quantity). Blueberries, for example, must be quick-blanched with a tea-kettle of boiling water to break down the natural wax coating that slows dehydration. Then they're a snap.

In arid climates, dehydration relies on clean, stacked screen racks that allow plenty of air circulation. Keep bugs and animals off the food by covering racks with lightweight agricultural cloth, muslin, or cheesecloth. Drying time can be several days, even with an outdoor temperature near 100 degrees F and very low humidity. In the rest of the country, solar dehydrators are popular as a do-it-yourself project. They magnify and concentrate the sun's power through a closed box containing racks.

Canning

Canning is old fashioned, and there's a reason the practice endures through generations. You can prepare and put up the entire harvest of a crop at one time, and once you're done in the kitchen you can enjoy the rewards all year—or for years—with no fuss and no storage cost. A bumper crop one year can balance out a bad harvest the next if you've got enough cans in the pantry.

Use canning for all kinds of products in addition to jams, jellies, and other fruit preserves: juices and syrups, whole or sauced fruit, and even pickled grape leaves.

Preserving food by canning shouldn't be a mystery, although some people are needlessly frightened of food poisoning. Dangerous botulism microorganisms can only grow in an air-less low-acid environment—vegetables, mostly—but all the high-acid fruits and any foods pickled in acidic brine are safe if correctly processed.

Still, canning is all about sanitation and creating a sterile environment that prevents the growth of any other bacterium, mold, or yeast. And that means learning to wash and steril-ize every jar, lid, and cooking implement you handle. Follow cooking and processing instructions carefully, being sure to check for applicable high-altitude adjustments to cooking time.

Canning requires some investment in equipment, including kettles for cooking and for the boiling-water processing bath; strainers, sieves, wide-mouth funnels, and cheesecloth; mea-suring cups and a food scale; and canning-size tongs. Then you have them forever. Heat-tempered canning jars come in sizes from a half cup to a half gallon, and these are reusable. Bands and lids should be replaced.

Use only ripe, unblemished produce for canning, and pick through and rinse it carefully to remove stems, bugs, dust, and so on (a few fruit recipes call for stems left on for pectin content).

In general, making preserves involves cooking fruit to soften the pulp and extract juice, and then adding sugar and cook-ing again to the jelling point. The jars are filled, sealed, and submerged in boiling water to kill germs and create a vacuum seal.

If the idea of using a lot of sugar is offensive, canning may not be for you. Sugar not only enhances flavor, but it is important in creating the "jell" in jelly and other preserves, and it is part of the preservative process too. There are no-sugar and reduced-sugar recipes, but results vary.

For easy beginners' canning recipes, see Nan's Blueberry Jam (page 48), Crabapple Jelly (page 22), and Rose Water Plum Compote (page 34).

Harvest time may last for months as edible landscape gardeners develop their skills. Orchard fruits, berries, even herbs go into the larder. Photo by www. rebeccadangelo photography.com.

Pressing and Fermentation

Making cider or fruit juice from orchard crops like apples, pears, and grapes is a delight: family or neighborhood groups can make a celebration of pressing fruit, since it takes many hands and many hours and produces large quantities of finished product. Perfect for sharing!

Cider can be refrigerated and consumed fresh, or pasteurized (heated briefly to a high temperature, but well below boiling) and then canned, or left unpasteurized to ferment. The same applies to grapes, which, incidentally, make a good mixer with other homemade fruit juices.

Making fresh fruit juices does not require a juicer. Just extract the juice by pressing or cutting fruit into pieces and cooking, just as for jams and jellies; let the liquid drip through a sieve and cheesecloth the same way. Omit the step of adding sugar and cooking to the jelling point. The heated—pasteurized—juice is then ready to can and seal in a hot water bath. Try mixing whatever is ripe at the same time into a single batch: grapes and pears, for instance, or crabapples and quince.

Cider making consists of two processes that are linked together in one mechanism: grinding the ripe fruit into chunks, and then squeezing batches of the chipped fruit (or whole fruit, in the case of grapes) with a screw press that fits into a loose wooden "basket." The juice runs freely into bowls or buckets below and can be further strained before processing. Never use stone fruits like peaches or cherries in a cider press, as they can ruin the grinder blades.

A cider press is a major investment, but with care it will last for many years. Simple fruit grinders begin at about $150, and grinder-press combinations range from about $600 to nearly $1,500; the most expensive have electric motors, but these can produce hundreds of gallons of fruit juice or cider in a day, rather than dozens of gallons with a hand-operated press.

Winemaking combines the sanitation requirements of canning with the temperature and handling practices of breadmaking. Once you get the hang of it, making wine is as simple as following any recipe. Wine uses almost no energy to produce, and it costs very little in supplies. Homemade wine makes a lovely gift and, of course, a delightful accompaniment to meals at home. There's a one-time investment in equipment—complete kits cost under $200— or you may be able to share with other amateur winemakers locally.

Put aside visions of syrupy, too-sweet fruit wines. There's a world of delicate, delicious wines from all corners of the edible landscape; herbs and wildflowers, vine and nut leaves, and unusual fruits like quince, pomegranate, and lemon all can produce excellent wine. Apples and pears are famous as hard cider and "perry" wine. Now consider rose hip wine, sage wine, grape leaf wine, or almond wine. To your health!

The principle of winemaking is this: living yeast cells interact with sugar, converting it to alcohol. Sugar-laden fruits often have enough sugar for fermentation on their own, but low-sugar plants like herbs and wildflowers need sugar or honey added (wine sweetened with honey is called mead). Likewise, yeast occurs naturally in many fruits, but most often a small batch of activated yeast is added to the mix to kick-start the reaction and crowd out competing microorganisms. A packet of bread yeast will do.

Winemaking begins with standard proportions—gleaned from millennia of human experience—of water or juice, flavoring (fruit or other edible plant), sweetener, and yeast. The mixture must begin at a lukewarm temperature, just like bread, and then it is left undisturbed in a warm, dark place. The wine is "cooking," a process that may take several months as gas bubbles continue percolating.

When the yeast has digested enough sugar, it dies off and fermentation ends. The wine now clarifies as if by magic and can be bottled, aged, and enjoyed.

Winemaking can take care of any real surplus from the garden. One recipe calls for forty to fifty pounds of peaches, easily attainable with just a few healthy trees.

Are there disadvantages to winemaking? I can't think of one.

Photo by Nan K. Chase

Resources

Internet resources for plant information seem limitless, sometimes overwhelming; evaluate Web resources with a rating feature like The Garden Watchdog on www.davesgarden.com.

One reliable place to start for detailed localized information—state by state and county by county—is the United States Department of Agriculture's Cooperative Extension System: www.csrees .usda.gov/Extension/. The Master Gardener program is listed there as well.

For help getting started with canning, drying, freezing, and other ways to preserve the harvest, visit the National Center for Home Food Preservation, www.uga.edu/nchfp/. The Wisconsin-based company NESCO/American Harvest is a good source for easy-to-operate electric dehydrators, www.nesco.com, and there are detailed instructions on drying food at www.aces.uiuc.edu/vista /html_pubs/drying/dryfood.html. Oliso makes a compact vacuum sealer called a Frisper with reusable plastic storage bags, www.oliso.com.

For product information about cider presses and related equipment, see Correll Cider Presses, www.correllciderpresses.com, or Happy Valley Ranch, www.happyvalleyranch.com.

Hard-copy and Internet garden catalogues supply detailed information about edible plant selection and care. Consult sources like One Green World, www.onegreenworld.com; Millers Nurseries, www.millernurseries.com; the Home Orchard Society, www.home orchardsociety.org; California Rare Fruit Growers, Inc., www.crfg .org; the Herb Society of America, www.herbsociety.org; American Pomological Society, www.americanpomological.org; and other garden organizations.

For environmentally low-impact pest control solutions see Gardens Alive!, www.gardensalive.com.

Shop at used bookstores for timeless advice on all garden topics, including "putting up" the harvest in various ways.

Consider joining a local garden club for education about local plants of value in the edible landscape, and for companionship while learning; see www.gcamerica.org.

Below is a list of Web sites offering recipes, nutritional information, and much more.

When all is said and done, experience by trial and error is the best teacher.

Photo courtesy of U.S. Apple Association.

Favorite Fruits

APPLE

U.S. Apple Association, www.usapple.org

Apple Products Research & Education Council,
www.appleproducts.org

Michigan Apples, www.michiganapples.com

CHERRY

National Cherry Growers & Industries Foundation,
www.nationalcherries.com

Northwest Cherries, www.nwcherries.com

PEACH

California Tree Fruit Agreement, www.eatcaliforniafruit.com

Georgia Peach Commission, www.gapeaches.org

PEAR

Pear Bureau Northwest, www.usapears.com

PLUM

California Tree Fruit Agreement, www.eatcaliforniafruit.com

California Dried Plums, www.californiadriedplums.org

101 Cookbooks, www.101cookbooks.com

QUINCE

A Wee Bit of Cooking: A Scottish Food Blog,
www.teach77.wordpress.com

Nuts & Berries

GENERAL, INCLUDING CHESTNUT, HAZELNUT/FILBERT, PECAN, WALNUT (AND BUTTERNUT)

Northern Nut Growers Association, Inc., www.icserv.com/nnga/

ALMOND

Almond Board of California, www.almondsarein.com

BLUEBERRY

U.S. Highbush Blueberry Council, www.blueberrycouncil.com

CHESTNUT

The American Chestnut Foundation, www.acf.org

HAZELNUT/FILBERT

The Hazelnut Council, www.hazelnutcouncil.org

PECAN

National Pecan Shellers Association, www.ilovepecans.org
Georgia Pecan Commission, www.georgiapecansfit.org

WALNUT

California Walnuts, www.walnuts.org
The Walnut Council, www.walnutcouncil.org

Herbs & Vines

GENERAL, INCLUDING BAY TREE, NASTURTIUM, LAVENDER, MINT, ROSEMARY, THYME, AND SAGE

The Herb Society of America, searching individual herb names,
www.herbsociety.org

GRAPE

California Table Grape Commission, www.tablegrape.com
California Raisins, www.raisins.org
North Carolina Muscadine Grape Association,
www.ncmuscadine.org

KIWI

California Kiwifruit Commission, www.kiwifruit.org
ZESPRI™ Kiwifruit, www.zespri.com
California Rare Fruit Growers, Inc., www.crfg.org

LAVENDER

Mountain Farm, with recipes under Lavender Products section, www.mountainfarm.net

Mountainside Lavender Farm, www.mountainsidelavender.com

NASTURTIUM

Sunrise Seeds, www.sunriseseeds.com

Hot-Country Choices

GENERAL, INCLUDING FIG, OLIVE, POMEGRANATE

California Rare Fruit Growers, Inc., www.crfg.org

FIG

California Fresh Fig Growers Association, www.calfreshfigs.com

KUMQUAT

Kumquat Growers, Inc., www.kumquatgrowers.com

LEMON, LIME, ORANGE

Florida Citrus, www.floridajuice.com

OLIVE

Publication #8267, University of California, Division of Agriculture and Natural Resources, www.anrcatalog.ucdavis.edu

The Olive Oil Source, www.oliveoilsource.com

Photo © iStockPhoto/Paul Giamatti

Wildflowers

Wrapped in ice, a rose hip stays fresh out of doors. The surprising beauty of wild roses extends beyond the usual growing season. ©Peter Jordt/subrosa.dk.

Index

METRIC CONVERSION CHART

VOLUME MEASUREMENTS

U.S.	Metric
1 teaspoon	5 ml
1 tablespoon	15 ml
1/4 cup	60 ml
1/3 cup	75 ml
1/2 cup	125 ml
2/3 cup	150 ml
3/4 cup	175 ml
1 cup	250 ml

WEIGHT MEASUREMENTS

U.S.	Metric
1/2 ounce	15 g
1 ounce	30 g
3 ounces	90 g
4 ounces	115 g
8 ounces	225 g
12 ounces	350 g
1 pound	450 g
2 1/4 pounds	1 kg

TEMPERATURE CONVERSION

Fahrenheit	Celsius
250	120
300	150
325	160
350	180
375	190
400	200
425	220
450	230